Small Talk that Doesn't Suck:

Stop Talking About the Weather & Start Making Real Connections

By Patrick King
Social Interaction and Conversation
Coach at
www.PatrickKingConsulting.com

Table of Contents

Chapter 1: Laying a Good Foundation

Have you ever heard someone say, "I love small talk! I can't get enough of it"?

Probably not, and yet small talk is actually one of humanity's greatest inventions. Small talk lowers risk while maximizing the chances of understanding and enjoyment. Small talk helps us connect with minimal fuss and hassle and makes sure that those initial interactions with a stranger are as rewarding as they possibly can be. Small talk is like a key—and it opens doors to more interesting conversations, more authentic relationships, and a life with far fewer misunderstandings.

This book is not just about *surviving* small talk or finding some clever hacks to help you avoid it. Instead, we'll be looking at ways to embrace and maximize this peculiar mode of interaction so that you genuinely can become that person who loves small talk.

In the chapters that follow, we'll be looking at the deeper attitudes and core beliefs that will actually empower and inspire you in social situations. We'll look at all the principles that will help you work with conversational energy and flow, lean into real curiosity for others, and show up in conversations as the real, unique, and vulnerable person you are right now. We'll also consider in some detail exactly what you say, when and how you say it, and what to do when things don't quite go to plan.

You may not feel much love for small talk right now (or indeed, any form of social interaction). Nevertheless, my hope is that by the end of this book, you will have found a renewed sense of appreciation for all the possibilities this art form can offer—and conversation is most definitely an art form!

Awkwardness Is not a Bug; It's a Feature

What's the number one reason people hate small talk? That's easy: It's awkward. It's cringey and embarrassing and super uncomfortable, right?

I'm here to tell you the good and the bad news. The bad news is that awkwardness really is an obstacle to enjoyable, easy conversation with others. But the good news is that it's a *psychological obstacle*—one that can be overcome.

Most of us could stand to connect more with those around us and have deeper and richer relationships with the people who are already in our worlds. We may recognize the desire to have better relationships and to connect more freely and comfortably with others, but the barrier to entry just seems way too high. We may look at the prospect of engaging with strangers and think, "That's too much hard work. It's just not worth it."

The first major mindset shift to make, however, is knowing how to honestly acknowledge awkwardness, to understand what it is, and to know how to communicate anyway. In other words, if you're unwilling to make social efforts until you feel less awkward . . . you'll be waiting a long time! Rather, the trick is to change the way you think about this feeling of awkwardness.

Ty Tashiro is a psychologist who was so interested in the phenomenon of awkwardness that he wrote a book about it, *Awkward: The Science of Why We're Socially Awkward and Why That's Awesome.* He describes awkwardness as a high-activation emotion characterized by discomfort and disorientation.

Tashiro explores a different approach: Feeling shy or a little uncomfortable is not actually the problem; rather, allowing these feelings to interfere with your ability to connect genuinely **is** the problem. Usually, our awkwardness stems from a minor deviation from what we consider normal socially; then, we overreact emotionally, making this minor deviation mean more than it should.

If our feelings of shyness and discomfort mean we avoid others, we create a reinforcing cycle: The less we put ourselves out there, the less practice we get and the more awkward we feel. But the more awkward we feel, the harder and harder it is to put ourselves out there.

He explains how awkward individuals often approach social situations with heightened sensitivity and self-awareness, which can lead to anxiety and overthinking. The way out is not to learn to get rid of these (perfectly normal) feelings, but rather to practice a little empathy and understanding, not just for ourselves but for others who might be struggling with social interactions (hint: that's most of us!).

Social anxiety is often accompanied by a whole host of negative assumptions, biases, and core beliefs. It's these assumptions that most get in the way—not other people per se. Do you subscribe to any of these assumptions and beliefs?

- People who are good at small talk just do it naturally and automatically.
- I am unique in finding socializing difficult and awkward.
- Finding small talk difficult and awkward is a good reason to avoid it.
- Small talk gets in the way of having "real" conversations.
- It's not possible to improve your social skills.
- Small talk is boring, unpleasant, and unnecessary—i.e., it's something you can just opt out of.
- Small talk is superficial, unintelligent, irrelevant.
- There is just no way to make small talk pleasant. It's a necessary evil.
- And many more . . .

But are any of these assumptions really true?

Take Ben, for example, who absolutely loathes small talk. He avoids it when he can. He hates that feeling of being mid-conversation with a stranger and not knowing what to say next. He hates the weird silences. It almost feels like being thrown into a pool when you don't know how to swim!

So, he concludes that small talk is just something he'll never enjoy and get better at. Had he realized, however, that a little weirdness and discomfort is actually not unusual, then he wouldn't have interpreted those silences in such a rigid, negative way. What's more, his core beliefs and assumptions about what small talk is supposed to feel like means he expects that it should come easily and naturally, with no effort.

Turning up to a social interaction without having prepared for it is like waking up one day and immediately starting a marathon. To extend this further, hating small talk is a little like getting a running injury because you're not warmed up, and then saying, "Running is boring and stupid. I hate it."

Without any planning or "warm-up," there are going to be injuries! Tashiro emphasizes the importance of *deliberate preparation* for social interactions, likening it to developing "social algorithms." This may go against a major assumption that we should find small talk automatic, easy, or spontaneous.

By anticipating and planning responses to common social scenarios, people can mitigate feelings of awkwardness and navigate interactions more smoothly. This proactive approach can empower you to engage with others confidently and authentically—in fact, simply taking charge of the situation and taking action to prepare is often enough on its own to make you feel calmer and more in control. One final suggestion from Tashiro is also counterintuitive: rather than being polite, restrained, and conventional, we should actually be *bold*.

Let's take a closer look at his tips for combatting inevitable social awkwardness.

Prepare Mentally for Social Situations

Consider adopting a strategy of mental preparation before entering social situations. Take the time to discuss and simulate potential scenarios in your head, such as ordering food at a restaurant—this is literally your social and conversational "warm-up." In your own time, guide yourself through the steps involved. In our example, this could mean noticing cues to interact politely with waitstaff.

What are the many little expectations you're going to encounter in this situation? And what are the behaviors that you need to do to feel socially at ease in that situation? Then prepare yourself accordingly. "What's the first thing I need to look for when I walk inside?" or "What do I need to do when I reach the cashier?"

Yes, rehearsing things in this way may itself feel a little awkward at first, but rest assured that it's not as unusual as you think. Imagine a stage actor or news presenter. They appear at complete ease and in control of their delivery, posture, and tone. That's no accident, however—these people have likely spent at least twenty minutes beforehand warming up their vocal cords, practicing facial expressions, and rehearsing lines. Your goal, of course, is not to put on a performance; nevertheless, the appearance of spontaneity can sometimes take a lot of preparation!

As you prepare mentally, you probably can't help but prepare emotionally, too. Give yourself a little pep talk and get in the right frame of mind. Tashiro tells *The Atlantic* magazine:

> *"I just have a little self-talk before I go into these situations. I call it my mental preparation, and I'll just say, 'Hey, you don't know anybody; you're nervous about that. And that's okay. You've been in these situations before, and you can do it.' But I need to have a more assertive attitude than would be natural for me."*

Many of us already ruminate anxiously before a social event; why not put all that brainpower to use and instead talk yourself up?

Create Social Scripts

People are unpredictable, and by extension that means that social situations are also unpredictable. However, you can go a long way to identify the most common social situations you're likely to encounter in your life, when, and where. Then, you can prepare by building potential scripts to use in those situations. Consider, for example, who you are most likely to encounter on a typical day, and what kind of interactions are probable. Then, anticipate things like greetings, introductions, and conversation starts in your mind.

In a similar way, try to pre-emptively identify those situations or dynamics that are most challenging for you. For example, if you already know that you find goodbyes the most excruciating part of an interaction, then pay special attention to your wording and demeanor during these moments. If meeting new people at work is the most difficult, then try to clearly visualize the precise details of such an interaction and prepare a simple script ahead of time.

Of course, nobody would suggest literally memorizing a script verbatim. *That* would be awkward! Don't worry that preparation of this kind makes you unspontaneous or inauthentic. Instead, think of these social scripts as a framework for navigating interactions smoothly. It's what keeps your anxiety out of the way enough *so that you can be* more spontaneous and authentic.

Be Bold in Social Interactions

Tashiro's final piece of advice is to take the initiative to approach others confidently. When we're anxious, we often inadvertently place ourselves in a passive, reactive frame of mind. We start to see social interaction as something that happens to us, something that other people do, and something we merely tolerate or endure.

The irony is that if we actively approach the source of our anxiety . . . much of that anxiety disappears. That's because we are no longer at the mercy of some external force, but rather active players in how the dynamic unfolds. If a stranger enters your periphery, immediately grab the chance to say hello (having a short "introduction social script" will come in extremely handy!). Simply say, "Hey, I'm [Your Name]. I'm new here. Do you mind if I join you?"

Although it might feel daunting at first, you'll often find that people are welcoming and receptive to your approach. Any nerves will often subside within seconds. The real awkwardness comes in acknowledging a potential moment of engagement . . . and then prolonging it. Instead, just dive in and don't draw things out. Be bold.

Returning to our original list of assumptions and core beliefs, let's rewrite them a little:

- Humans are built to connect socially, but that doesn't mean that it comes automatically or that it's always easy.
- Social awkwardness is more common than you think.
- Just because someone feels socially awkward at times doesn't mean they can never approach others, make friends, or connect in conversations.
- Small talk is not something we do instead of "real" conversations, but something we do to build up to more closeness and connection.
- No matter where you're starting from, everyone can improve their social skills.
- Small talk is *not* superficial, unintelligent, or irrelevant, but an indispensable and highly valuable life skill.
- There's nothing small about small talk—it can be enjoyable and meaningful (yes, really!).

- Scripting and preparing for social interactions are a proactive way to get better at small talk—as well as manage anxiety.

Remember: It's Not Just About You

Jenny suffers from social anxiety. She's always felt extremely self-conscious in conversations—particularly in groups or parties. It's become enough of a problem that Jenny realizes she has to make changes. So, she thinks to herself, *How can I be a better communicator? How can I improve my social skills? How can I become a more interesting and likeable person? Should I change my appearance in any way? Should I learn a few jokes that people will find funny? What exactly do you do if you want to come across as charming or charismatic . . .?*

These thoughts are natural enough, and you've probably asked yourself similar questions when feeling socially nervous, anxious, or unconfident.

Look back at Jenny's stream of thoughts, however, and you'll see something interesting: It's all about her. How interesting or charming or funny she is. What she should say and when and how.

In fact, self-consciousness and social anxiety are both heavily associated with this kind of inward focus. The trouble is, when your awareness is turned inward this way, you are no longer paying close attention to the external world and all the unique, interesting people in it. And so, by worrying about how you're coming across socially . . . you come across badly!

One fundamental perspective switch to make is to realize that small talk—or any kind of conversation—is not just about you. It involves you, and you are certainly playing a role as one of the co-creators of that situation. But it is not *about* you—people have not assembled exclusively to listen to your jokes and decide whether they're funny or not, or rate you according to how intelligent or charming you seem (unless, of course, you're a stand-up comedian or a contestant in a beauty pageant!).

Once we realize that social interactions are not about shining the limelight on us and us alone, then we're free to do something more important: pay attention to the other person. We can become curious about them, we can ask questions, and we can be interested, respectful, and attentive listeners. The great thing about this is that it's so much less anxiety-provoking.

Personalize Your Communication

Personalized communication, in the context of marketing, refers to the process of tailoring interactions, messages, and experiences to individual customers or prospects based on data collected about them. This tailored approach aims to enhance the overall customer experience and foster a deeper connection between the company and the individual.

What has that got to do with becoming better at small talk?

Well, marketers are experts at communication (if they're good marketers, that is), and their skill lies in understanding that the effectiveness of communication rests entirely on how *targeted* it is. Your message can be as interesting, factually correct, intelligent, or entertaining as humanly possible, but if it's delivered in a way that the other person can't connect with, then it won't work. Communication fails.

Personalizing your communication means knowing that there is no one right way to make small talk. There isn't a universal joke, anecdote, or question. Rather, what works is what works for the person in front of you.

Socially skilled people understand that they have to tailor their communication to suit the preferences, interests, behaviors, and characteristics of every individual they talk to. Just as a friend who gives you a personalized gift demonstrates their understanding and care for you, personalizing your communication shows that you not only acknowledge that person's uniqueness, but that you respect it, too.

In the context of small talk, personalization refers to steering the conversation toward topics that are more intimate or directly related to either yourself or your conversation partner. Small talk often *seems* very generic, but scratch the surface of a good small talk interaction and you will see that even the most superficial topics can be gently tailored to suit the people involved.

By the way, "superficial" does not necessarily mean impersonal or trivial. You can have a quick, light conversation that is nevertheless filled with warmth, connection, and kindness. Just because it's small talk doesn't mean you have to limit yourself to a dry discussion about local news or the weather. A more personalized conversation is naturally going to be a more *personal* one—and personal conversations have the power to create emotional bonds because they involve sharing thoughts, memories, and feelings. All of this can be done in even a brief, superficial moment of small talk.

Personalization in small talk is essential for building rapport and deepening connections between people. It allows for a more meaningful exchange that goes beyond surface-level interactions, ultimately fostering stronger relationships. Making things personal is the bridge that carries you from the initial awkwardness of being strangers to more comfortable and familiar states.

How do you gently start to make conversations feel more personal?

Ask About Wants/Pursuits/Tendencies

By inquiring about someone's desires, activities, or habits, you're inviting them to share personal aspects of their life. This demonstrates genuine interest in understanding the other person beyond surface-level interactions.

You: "So, what's your favorite thing to do at the beach?"

Them: "I really love surfing and just soaking up the sun. How about you?"

You: "Surfing, wow! I'm more of a beachcomber myself, always searching for interesting seashells and taking long walks along the shore."

What to avoid:

- Sharing personal details about yourself is not wrong, but it's usually more effective to show an interest in them first.
- Remember that small talk is not about exchanging useful information; it's not a practical interaction but a social one. Avoid getting stuck sharing facts and data for too long. Instead, ask what that data *means* to the other person.

Ask About Plans

While slightly less personal than desires, asking about someone's plans still encourages them to open up about their intentions and activities. It can serve as a springboard to more intimate topics and provide insights into their interests and priorities. A conversation about plans is never too far from a conversation about dreams, goals, motivations, and values.

You: "What brings you out today?"

Them: "I'm meeting some friends for coffee. How about you?"

You: "I'm just exploring the neighborhood. But I know the coffee here's really good!"

What to avoid:

- Keep questions small and light—you don't want to come across as interrogating people or demanding they explain themselves.
- As tempting as it is, avoid "Any plans for the weekend?" Broad, open-ended questions may put people on the spot and invite generic answers (more on this in a later chapter). Focus initially on closed questions that will be easier to answer. "We're getting a dog." "Oh, that's great. Any plans for a name?"

Reference the Other Person in Your Examples

Incorporating the other person into your anecdotes or observations not only makes them feel included but also prompts them to reflect on their own experiences and preferences. This is a sneaky but powerful way to show them that you're listening.

For example, let's say you already know that the person you're talking to is a nurse. You might be telling them a casual anecdote about your new dog, and you say, "He's been so sick right now, but he completely refuses to take his medicine. He doesn't know we're only trying to help him—that's probably something *you're* familiar with, being a nurse, right?"

Make Everything About How It Affects Them

Okay, maybe not *everything*. But showing empathy and concern for how situations might impact the other person demonstrates attentiveness and fosters deeper emotional connections. It encourages them to share their feelings and experiences, further enhancing rapport. It also showcases you as a trustworthy, empathetic person.

For example, you're at a busy event in a big auditorium. You notice that the person you've just been introduced to is wearing very high heels and appears to be uncomfortable in them. Though you're not struggling yourself, you remark on the shoes and casually suggest you both find somewhere to sit.

With just this simple observation and suggestion, you convey not only that you noticed their discomfort, but also that it mattered to you. What's more, there's now an invitation to talk about something a little more personal—perhaps how much they love high heels but always regret wearing them! Such an interaction may not seem like a big deal, but little courtesies like this one can be hugely impactful—and they're only possible if you're not too focused on your own experience.

Try to Relate and Be Relatable

Finding common ground or expressing empathy with the other person's interests or experiences strengthens the connection between both parties. Sharing relatable aspects of your own life also encourages reciprocity and a deeper exchange of personal information.

Them: "Helping animals is my passion."

You: "Wow, that's admirable. I've never been an animal person myself, but I do volunteer at the children's hospital, and I get so much satisfaction out of that. It feels good to help."

In this example, you can see how the response is ever so slightly tailored to send the unspoken message "you and I are similar." Compare it to:

Them: "Helping animals is my passion."

You: "Wow, I couldn't do it. I don't like dogs. Or cats, actually."

Consciously drawing connections between you and other people not only creates strong rapport, it also just leads to far more interesting and flowing dialogue.

Speak Their Language

Finally, the best way to speak to someone is to use the kind of language you know they'll be most receptive to hearing. Now, this takes imagination and empathy (we'll talk about empathy a lot more in a later chapter), but an easy way to understand the best language with which to speak to someone is to listen to what they say to you—then use that language yourself.

Work with Conversational Energy

Conversational energy is the intangible yet palpable quality that influences how people feel during interactions. It's a little like "chemistry" except platonic, and it's one of those things that's very easy to feel, yet quite tricky to put your finger on.

This kind of energy serves as fuel for small talk by infusing it with vitality, enthusiasm, and genuine interest, but it's also the result of good rapport. When people engage in small talk with just the right energy and "vibe," they create an engaging and uplifting atmosphere, making the conversation more enjoyable for both parties. Good energy allows people to connect more easily, smooth over misunderstandings and friction, and build stronger, more enjoyable relationships.

Conversely, small talk with low or poor energy can make everything feel dull and uninspiring. This is why people "hate small talk." They feel uninspired or outright uncomfortable, and they want to disengage but feel they can't. The entire interaction takes on a tone of force, mild resentment, or boredom. Unfortunately, feeling that way tends to make connecting even harder, and you're soon stuck with a vicious cycle of reinforcing tedium.

The good news is that conversational energy isn't some mysterious force gifted to you by the muses; it's something you can learn to conjure deliberately, and with just a little practice you can inject enough life and vibrancy into short exchanges that they can "launch" and run on their own steam.

The secret to creating conversational energy is to create **variety and dynamism**.

You want movement and variability in what you say and how you say it. One area where variability is important is in the tone of your voice. Listening to a monotone voice is like riding a boring roller coaster. Actually, it's not a roller coaster at all, but one of those boring train rides for kids: going nowhere slowly on a flat, straight track. Think of Toby Flenderson from *The Office*—he's a prime example of how *not* to talk. If your voice sounds anything like his, chances are people won't enjoy listening to you.

Make sure your voice has energy and variation to keep people interested. Make it move from one pitch to another. Change your pace and speed. Articulate yourself. Add color and interest to your delivery by varying your volume, sentence length, or expression so that what you're saying takes on dimension and richness. If you sound like you're reading the dictionary to a sleeping cat, don't be surprised if others tune out or change the topic.

Sometimes we can mistakenly think that talking is just a method for dispensing information. We get stuck on the idea of *what* we say and forget that *how* we say it matters just as much, if not more. Remember those times when you felt socially awkward? Your nervousness might have made your breathing a little irregular and shallow. This in turn might have made your voice come across as weak, too quiet, or shaky sounding.

Nervousness can make people rush or mumble. If you're coming across as unconfident, people may respond in certain ways that make you feel even less sure of yourself. For example, if you are shy and speak quietly, the conversational energy slows and lowers, and you may find that interest quickly fizzles out—it's that vicious circle again.

So how do you ever improve? First, keep reminding yourself that what you say matters less than how you say it. Don't get too hung up on saying the "right" thing, and don't worry about rehearsing or delivering a perfect speech. Think right now of someone you consider to be an effective speaker. Chances are you seldom remember the exact words they say, but their demeanor and attitude certainly leaves a lasting impression. Interesting people aren't just smart or accurate—they speak with energy and enthusiasm. Take the pressure off yourself by remembering that you don't need to be a rock star to be engaging.

Cultivating a Dynamic, Engaging Voice

Embracing vocal variation can initially feel strange at first because it's different from what feels normal. It may feel too obvious, too deliberate, even a little cheesy. This goes back to our core beliefs about social interactions, specifically that communicating should be easy and effortless, and that we shouldn't need to spend any time to prepare or practice. Sometimes we can unconsciously assume that if *we* know what we mean and intend to communicate, then others should just magically "get" that without us having to try too hard to explain.

Over the Covid pandemic, many people found themselves retreating into their homes and spending far, far less time socializing. They discovered with some surprise that going back into the social world after being in lockdown was challenging. When talking to people, they now felt rusty, awkward, and out of practice— because they were!

When you wake up in the morning, your voice is probably hoarse and a little croaky because your vocal cords have been dormant all night. Having low vocal variety and dynamism is similar—it will feel awkward at first because you're simply not warmed up.

Here are some ways that you can loosen up your voice and start getting used to bringing more color and dynamism into the way you speak.

Activity 1: Mirror Exercise

Stand in front of a mirror, choose a phrase or sentence, and practice saying it with different tones of voice to convey various emotions. Observe your facial expressions and body language as you speak. What do you notice?

You can start with the phrase "I'm really excited about this opportunity." Say it with a tone of enthusiasm to convey excitement, then try saying it with a calm tone to convey sincerity. How do small differences in facial and vocal expression change how you come across?

The great thing about doing this in a mirror is that you see what others see. We are always in our own head, and this creates a kind of blind spot; we feel something and just assume that other people know what we're feeling. But they can't, unless we're expressing or conveying that in some way, right? People don't respond to the *words* "I'm excited." They respond to your lifted eyebrows, wide-open eyes, and elevated tone of voice.

You can also try imitating cartoon characters, practicing tongue twisters, or even doing impressions of famous actors delivering noteworthy lines from movies. How would you say XYZ if you were an actor in a movie playing that role? How could you best convey exactly the right message? What you're doing is experimenting with all the ways that your delivery influences how you're perceived.

Activity 2: Emotion Charades

Write down a list of emotions, choose one randomly, and without speaking any words, try to convey that emotion through your tone of voice. Can you think of gestures, body postures, and facial expressions that could emphasize the expression of this emotion? You could even try having others guess the emotion based solely on your vocal expression.

Choose the emotion "frustration" and express it through your tone of voice by using a slightly raised pitch, faster pace, and slight intensity, without using any words. It's quite fun to choose completely neutral or random words unconnected to the emotion.

A variation of this game is to watch films or video clips in a language you don't understand, or else watch them with the sound muted. This forces you to pay attention to nonverbal expressions. What nonverbal elements can you include in your own communication?

Activity 3: Tone of Voice Journaling

If you find vocal expression particularly challenging, you might enjoy keeping a journal dedicated to your tone of voice. After each verbal interaction, reflect on your tone and its appropriateness, effectiveness, and impact on others. Write down your observations and insights.

After a meeting, for example, reflect on whether your tone was assertive enough when presenting ideas and if it encouraged collaboration among team members. How was your volume, pitch, and speed? Did you make effective use of things like facial expression and body language?

Using a journal is a good way to keep track of what actually works for you. If you find socializing difficult, you may not sincerely believe that small changes like this can make a difference, but if you deliberately keep track of your effectiveness in a journal, you may prove to yourself just how important small variations can be.

Activity 4: Role-Play Scenarios

Create scenarios or conversations, pair up with someone, and take turns playing different roles. Many people do this kind of thing for fun, anyway—especially children! Focus on using appropriate tones of voice for each role and situation and throw yourself into your make-believe role. If possible, ask for feedback from the other person—what message did they receive? What exactly gave them that impression? If you're one of those people who is constantly misunderstood (for example, you're happy but people think you're angry or sad), then prepare to be surprised with this exercise!

You could role-play a customer service interaction where one person plays the customer with a complaint and the other plays the customer service representative, using a calm and empathetic tone to resolve the issue. You could role-play a radio talk show, a job interview, a first date, a bit of small talk at the bus stop, or anything else you can think of.

Activity 5: Storytelling

There's a reason stories play such a big role in children's education: Stories help us understand the rhythms and flows of narrative, and they teach us empathy, emotional literacy, and perspective-taking. When kids engage with a story, they are really learning how to socialize, how to play a role, and the rules of human communication.

You can use stories to help improve your own verbal articulation and expression. Pick a story to read out loud—and yes, a kid's story will often be a good choice! As you read, pay close attention to how you're breathing and modulating your voice. Pace yourself and take care to change your pitch, volume, and tone depending on what you're trying to convey. Change your voice entirely when reading parts for other characters, and be as theatrical as you can. Really imagine that you are trying to enthrall and entertain a young child (if possible, find a real young child to practice with).

The point of these exercises is simply to help you become more aware of how your voice influences your communication and how others perceive you. This way, you learn to modulate your voice to better express yourself in various situations.

The Secret Recipe: Add Salt, Fat, Acid, and Heat to Conversations

Renowned chef Samin Nosrat's culinary philosophy of "salt, acid, fat, and heat" can also be used to enhance the quality of our conversations. If we understand any human interaction as a kind of dish, we can start to look at it in terms of its ingredients—is it too bland and boring? A little on the spicy side? Or just right and absolutely delicious?

The elements of salt, fat, acid, and heat symbolize the essential components in conversation analogous to their roles in cooking. In the same way that we can adjust a lackluster dish by adding any of these four elements, we can elevate our conversational skills for more "tasty" interactions. Let's take a look.

Adding Salt

A meal without salt is . . . fine. But salt always adds a sharp, sparkling quality to food, and just a little is needed.

The element of salt in conversation represents the humor, wit, and charm that can make a conversation engaging and enjoyable. *Just a pinch* of humor or wit can add flavor and interest to a conversation. More than a pinch and it can quickly overwhelm.

To integrate the "salt" element into your conversations, use well-timed jokes or amusing observations to lighten the atmosphere and cultivate a livelier conversation. For instance, sharing a funny anecdote related to the topic at hand can break the ice and foster a sense of camaraderie.

Introduce clever wordplay or witty remarks to sustain engagement and pique interest. A cleverly phrased response or a humorous twist on a familiar topic can stimulate conversation and keep it dynamic. Remember that you don't need to suddenly be a hilarious stand-up comedian—just a sprinkle of light humor is often more than enough.

The active dose of salt/humor is in fact so low that you can achieve this effect merely by *suggesting* humor, without necessarily being funny. Employ a warm demeanor, try a friendly tone, or use genuine compliments to enhance the conversational experience. Initiating conversations with a sincere smile or offering thoughtful compliments can create a welcoming environment and facilitate meaningful connections. A lighthearted, silly, or playful demeanor is in many cases more effective than a literal joke with a punchline!

Adding Acid

Sometimes the most delicious food has a little edge of sourness to it. In just the right quantities, the cold burn of something sour is registered as pleasant and refreshing. Just like salt, however, the dose is what matters.

Conversational "acid" can be understood as things like curiosity, skepticism, and critical thinking, which contribute to "sharp" and stimulating discussions. Incorporating curiosity or skepticism into dialogue adds a tangy and invigorating quality to conversations. It's the unexpected element that makes things feel fresh, novel, and a little zesty.

One way to include a little acid is to lean a little into curiosity. By asking open-ended questions and demonstrating genuine interest in the other person's viewpoints, one keeps the dialogue dynamic and avoids stagnation. Dial this up by asking an entirely unpredictable question—it's like a breath of fresh air (or a squirt of lemon juice?) into a stale conversation.

Additionally, infusing a hint of skepticism can invigorate discussions by challenging assumptions. Follow-up questions and probing inquiries help add layers to the conversation, preventing it from becoming one-sided and encouraging deeper exploration of topics. A little friction and playful disagreement can stop the interaction from becoming too formulaic. For example, someone can say something a little controversial or confusing. It's as though everyone's ears prick a little when they hear this. Engagement and interest go through the roof—we are no longer going through the motions!

Critical thinking, analyzing arguments, providing counterpoints, and offering alternative perspectives all stimulate more profound and meaningful discussions, enriching the overall exchange. Of course, be aware that too much acid makes you come across as hot-tempered, argumentative, or domineering.

Adding Fat

In our extended metaphor, fat represents lovely, soothing qualities like empathy, vulnerability, and emotional intelligence, which imbue discussions with depth and sincerity. Just as fat enriches dishes and makes them comforting and nourishing, these attributes contribute richness and meaning to conversations.

Unlike salt and acid, you can get away with quite a bit of fat. Use the warmth of empathy to cultivate a compassionate environment by demonstrating understanding and resonance with the other person's emotions. Foster authenticity and connection by introducing feelings and emotions. Express vulnerability by openly sharing personal thoughts and feelings, and create trust and intimacy by respecting and accepting other people's emotional expression.

Emotional communication, like fat, is a kind of lubricant. It helps soothe over misunderstandings, mismatches, and miscommunications. If an interaction is feeling a little dry or thin, then inject some empathy and humanity into things. Reveal a teeny tiny secret about yourself, talk about your emotions, or enquire about theirs. Just remember that there is such a thing as too much empathy and emotion. Too much fat can make things feel sluggish and heavy. A good trick is to lighten any overly heavy emotional moments with a dash of humor for balance.

Adding Heat

Heat in conversation embodies passion, enthusiasm, and excitement, infusing discussions with energy and dynamism. Analogous to how heat enhances flavor in cooking, these qualities energize and invigorate dialogue. It's easy to imagine that too much heat can actually create a dish that is too hot, or a conversation that is too stimulating. If you've ever been in a "heated debate" that started as a simple conversation, you'll know how quickly this can happen.

Passion will infuse a conversation with energy and enthusiasm. Sharing your excitement about a topic can ignite the interest of the other person and keep them engaged—and they certainly don't need to share or agree with your passion to benefit from that boost in energy. Too many of us hang back and refrain from sharing our quirky interests, our big loves, or our unconventional obsessions. We think that people would prefer to hear a more sanitized, conventional opinion. The truth is, however, that a little injection of real enthusiasm can be like jet fuel for a conversation, not to mention it creates intimacy and a sense of realness.

Have you ever been in a friendship with someone for years and years, and yet you still felt like you didn't really *know* them? Chances are, they never fully shared their deepest, most unique passions with you. Being brave enough to show a little of your true self in conversations will not only make you seem more interesting, but it will capture people's attention and lower a few barriers of formality.

Now, this metaphor is kind of neat on paper, but in real life, it will take some practice to put to good use. One way to do this is to learn to be mindful in conversations as they're unfolding. Ask yourself internally, **What's missing here?** Then think of ways you can add just a little dash of the lacking ingredient to bring more balance.

For example, you may find yourself trapped in a very dull and superficial conversation with someone new—a fellow student on a weekend course you're taking. There is a back-and-forth, and there are no awkward silences, but at the same time there is very little conversational energy and it all feels a bit safe, a bit predictable, and a bit boring. You ask yourself what's missing, and you realize: it's *specificity*. You two are having a conversation that anyone could have anywhere in the world. In fact, you feel like you've already had this conversation millions of times before.

Being mindful of this, you try to think of ways to inject something new, unique, and completely special into the dynamic. You lean in and say in an over-the-top, conspiratorial voice, "Just between you and me, I'm only doing this course because I heard they give you donuts at the end," then wink like you're in a cheesy seventies' spy movie. It's completely silly, but it will instantly change the tone of the conversation—a little salt and heat to add interest.

In the same way, being mindful of the existing elements of an unfolding conversation helps you avoid adding more of what's already not working. For example, if you're in a conversation that is getting way too bogged down in emotional angst and oversharing, then it would be a bad move to dig even deeper and carry on being more earnest, sensitive, and serious. In the same way, a conversation that looks a little too heated or sour won't be improved by you adding more of your own energy, passion, or friction. Instead, quickly cool things off with some genuine sweetness and empathy.

Remember that your best tool for adding salt, acid, fat, or heat is not your words, but your voice:

- If you want to add salt/humor, then speed up your talking and make it lighter and brighter. Laugh or smile—you can always hear a smile in someone's voice.
- If you want to add acid/curiosity, then introduce a little darkness to your voice.

Raise it high to indicate a question or a questioning tone. Use pauses or sounds like "Hmmm . . ."

- If you want to add fat/empathy, then make your voice slower, softer, and gentler.
- If you want to add heat/passion, then increase your voice volume, pitch, and expressiveness.

Summary:

- Don't postpone making social efforts until you feel less awkward. Instead, accept and acknowledge awkwardness as a natural part of conversation.
- Don't allow awkwardness and anxiety to interfere with your ability to connect genuinely. Become curious about any biases, assumptions, or beliefs that are getting in the way—for example, the idea that we should find small talk automatic, easy, or spontaneous.
- Don't be afraid to prepare and practice for social interactions. Be bold, use social scripts and "algorithms," and prepare yourself mentally and emotionally before socializing.
- Social anxiety can make us turn inward and hyperfocus on ourselves, but this means we lose connection with others. Instead, externalize your awareness and show

curiosity about others. This will lower anxiety.

- There is no one right way to do small talk—you need to personalize your approach. Seek common ground or ask questions about more personal topics.
- The secret to creating conversational energy is to create variety and dynamism. How you speak is more important than what you say, so practice speaking with dynamism and a varied voice. Pay attention to your body language, expressions, and emotional articulation.
- The elements of salt, fat, acid, and heat symbolize the essential components in conversation analogous to their roles in cooking. Observe what a conversation is missing and add a little salt (humor, wit), fat (empathy, emotions), heat (passion and excitement), or acid (skepticism, curiosity) to improve it.

Chapter 2: The Secret of Brilliant Small Talk

Natalie was someone who had always struggled with social interactions, so when she received an autism diagnosis later in adulthood, a lot of pieces suddenly fell into place. The trouble was, Natalie found that the diagnosis actually made it harder to connect. She had always felt different; now she had concrete proof that she really was. She became concerned about whether others could "tell." She became obsessed with findings tricks and shortcuts to help her pass as "normal" and ensure that nobody could make out how difficult she found everything.

This plan only backfired. When Natalie met new people, she was so anxious about how she appeared to them that she quickly became overwhelmed and acted even more awkwardly than she normally would. It got so bad that

Natalie soon felt like giving up altogether. She soon had the attitude that she didn't care anymore about pretending to be someone she wasn't. But then, a curious thing happened. She suddenly found herself far, far more comfortable in social interactions—enjoying them, even. So, what happened?

Your Flaws Are Small Talk Material

People often avoid social interactions because they fear making mistakes or saying something silly. They fear looking like idiots, stumbling on their words, or having others notice that they are anxious. Like Natalie, they may genuinely believe that the only way they can become better at socializing is to become less of who they really are. They imagine that success means crafting some kind of perfect mask to put over their real selves so that nobody ever sees their awkward, uncomfortable, unusual selves.

The best conversationalists don't hide their flaws, however; instead, **they embrace them**. In fact, they have an attitude that does not see flaws at all, but rather simple variations. Being socially confident and having engaging conversations does not mean that we are perfect and untouchable. Instead, it actually begins with being vulnerable. This realization is often very counterintuitive for those who have spent much of their lives feeling like outsiders.

Vulnerability involves being open, admitting faults, and sharing hopes, failures, and fears while acknowledging weaknesses. It means being brave enough to lead with your own humanity—exactly as it is and exactly as you are.

Our culture often values stoicism, imperviousness, and superhuman success. Our collective model for a super accomplished extrovert is someone who seems kind of bulletproof and beyond reproach. These are the figures we see conjured before us in the form of glossy celebrities or social media influencers who are almost painfully perfect. They don't struggle, make fools of themselves, or feel bad. They're invincible and everything is easy for them, right?

Actually, this vision is worse than harmful—it's just plain wrong. A 1998 study on interpersonal vulnerability and anxiety revealed that individuals who express vulnerability and engage in open communication tend to have more positive social experiences and lower anxiety levels (Pincus, Gurtman, and Ruiz). In other words, being flawed and human makes you more successful at social interaction, not less.

Really pause and let that sink in a little.

Likable and easy-going individuals who make others feel comfortable typically embrace their character flaws and are comfortable in their skin. They are willing to be vulnerable and openly acknowledge their imperfections. These people readily admit they aren't perfect and are happy to laugh at their personal quirks, using their flaws to their advantage. Rather than their imperfections and weaknesses acting as a barrier to connection with others, they use these imperfections themselves to connect.

Consider the example from the previous chapter, where you playfully reveal that you only attended the weekend course because you heard there would be free donuts at the end. Yes, it's a silly joke, but it's also a subtle way of saying: "Hey, I'm not perfect. Sometimes I can be a little lazy/greedy/shameless, but I can own that and accept that about myself. I can laugh at it all, me included."

Contrast this to someone else you might meet at this weekend course who is dead serious and committed to the course. In fact, the way they list off their many other accomplishments is pretty intimidating. They're smart, attractive, and successful, and though you feel like you admire them . . . you also don't necessarily *connect* with them.

Natasha found this out for herself. By trying to come across as someone who had it all together (i.e., someone she wasn't!), she actually hid away her best "small talk material." In trying to convey a certain image of what she thought she should be, she missed out on the better opportunity (i.e., to show up as the person she really was).

How to Be "Confidently Vulnerable"

Forget everything you know about what it means to be a "confident" person. You can be relaxed, confident, and totally charming without being a loudmouth extrovert, without being dazzlingly funny and entertaining, and without being a supremely talented and impressive person. In fact, some of your best tools for genuine connection are things you already possess.

Embrace Your Weaknesses and Insecurities as Conversation Material

Instead of bragging about your successes, share amusing stories about your minor failures or embarrassing moments. Not only does this make for more engaging conversations, but it also makes others feel better about themselves. People are often drawn to those who can laugh at their flaws, because it shows a kind of maturity and emotional resilience that is very attractive.

For instance:

Nate: "Wow, that's an awesome handbag."

Lisa: "Thanks! Actually, I didn't pick it myself. It was a gift from my husband."

Nate: "Well, he's got great taste."

Lisa: "He does! Not like me, I've got awful taste. Maybe he didn't want to see what I'd pick for myself if left to my own devices!"

By admitting a "weakness," Lisa keeps the conversation interesting and playful. Sharing moments of vulnerability adds humility and depth to your interactions.

You can also start with these phrases:

I never knew _____.

I didn't expect that_____.

You probably shouldn't take my advice, but _____.

I'm the last person to _____.

I know absolutely nothing about _____.

Transform Awkward Moments into Lighthearted Ones by Acknowledging Your Imperfections

Just like all the world's best comedians, don't shy away from poking fun at yourself. For many famous people, in fact, their biggest flaw has been re-christened as their unique selling point and their most recognizable feature. For example, let's say you're in a car with your boss on the way to a conference, and you briefly mess up the directions. It's awkward for a moment, but then you laugh and playfully confess, "I'm sorry, I'm what they call navigationally impaired . . . If I say turn 'left,' I would strongly suggest turning right!"

Just like that you open up about a little weakness you have, but you also create a moment of bonding and good humor that smooths over any difficulty. The irony is that people who are open and upfront about their flaws are actually felt to be more trustworthy and likeable than those who have the same flaws but viciously deny it or try to hide it.

Use the Power of Self-deprecating Humor to Build Connections

Here are some examples:

"I can't believe I just did that! I think I left my brain at home today."

"Oh dear. You can see now why I'm not a world-famous artist, right?"

"Trust me, you don't want to try my cooking . . . Pretty sure I'm on a CIA terrorist list somewhere."

"We shouldn't take my car—the wheels will fall off halfway."

"Well, I'm not pretty, but my mother loves me. I think."

For a quirky twist when you say something odd, try: "That's just the first thing that popped into my head . . . I don't know why!" For an extra touch, add, "Can you tell I need to work on my internal filters?" When you embrace your imperfections and learn to turn mistakes into moments of humor, the fear diminishes.

According to author and shame expert Brené Brown, vulnerability is always key:

> *"Vulnerability is the birthplace of connection and the path to the feeling of worthiness. If it doesn't feel vulnerable, the sharing is probably not constructive."*

That doesn't mean we have to bare our souls or lunge into oversharing, however. We never want to dump our broken, imperfect selves on the other person as if to say, "Here I am! Take it or leave it!" Instead, it's a more subtle, more resilient attitude. We want to face vulnerability—our own and that of other people—with gentle acceptance. We don't have to hide or deny our flaws, but we also don't have to celebrate or wallow in them either. Instead, we can acknowledge them with a little humor and lenience, and not let them get in the way of our connection with others.

In the same way, self-deprecating humor needs to be more humor than it is self-deprecation. For example, you don't want to lay it on so thick that people genuinely start to worry whether you're beating yourself up for real. "I'm awful with directions. Truly, it's so embarrassing. You should just fire me and get it over with!" Everyone's humor levels are different, but you don't want to skirt so close to "dark humor" that it's hard to discern if you're serious or not.

In the same way, try not to use humor or self-deprecation or embrace your flaws when the matter is a serious one. A little levity is great for everyday frictions, but if you've made a serious error in judgment (i.e., you've crashed the car and totaled it), your best bet is likely to match the tone of the other person and take things seriously.

Don't Be Afraid to Share Your Opinions

Most people have heard the common etiquette advice to avoid talking about religion, politics, money, or sex in polite company. The funny thing is, of course, that these four topics also happen to be the things people are most interested in discussing!

Today more than ever, the world feels highly divisive and fractured—it is best to avoid it all, we are told, if we want to avoid conflict or awkwardness. It's not bad advice. After all, these topics are never far from strong opinions and deeply held convictions that can quickly lead people into arguments, misunderstandings, and hurt feelings.

The real skill, however, is not to avoid entire topics or refrain from sharing your opinion. This, predictably, will make your conversations impersonal and a little boring. Small talk should be safe and pleasant, yes, but that doesn't mean you cannot be real or show something of your authentic self.

Many of us treat our own opinions like sacred, precious possessions we are unwilling to ever part with. At the same time, we may see the opinions of others as unfortunate facts of life that we'd prefer to ignore or perhaps be "tolerant" of. Our culture frames opinions as all-or-nothing, right or wrong. Whether we know it or not, many of us have a knee-jerk reaction whenever we hear someone else's opinion (particularly if it differs from ours): We immediately try to determine whether we agree with it or not, whether we like it or not, whether it's right or wrong or worthy of our respect. It's not great to admit, but sometimes we see the sharing of a different opinion as an invitation to competition and conflict—i.e., whose opinion should "win"?

The truth is that it is the above attitude that leads to conflict—not differing opinions in themselves. Two people can differ wildly in their opinions and talk comfortably and pleasantly, and two people with an identical opinion can fight bitterly!

People who are master communicators, and those who are good at socializing and small talk, all have a very different mindset around opinions. They see other people's opinions as intrinsically valuable. When people share their opinions (that is, when they share *themselves*), it means that new ideas, new possibilities, and new energy can enter into an interaction. You suddenly have a dialogue and a back and forth. Things can move.

When people share opinions, they are allowing others to see and know them; their identity becomes more defined, and their values and perspectives are put out into the world—which means others can respond meaningfully. Without discussing and expressing opinions, personal and collective growth is hindered. People remain at a distance.

Master communicators think far beyond "everyone is entitled to their opinion."

We should not think of respect and acknowledgement of difference as a begrudging right, but rather the thing that makes people interesting, unique, and valuable. We all have preferences, perspectives, unique values and interests, goals, tastes, and personalities. Thinking that opinions are rights and that we need to tolerate the opinions of others misses the point—because the value of opinions is not in whether they are right or wrong. Opinions are not absolute truths but perspectives. Acknowledging these diverse viewpoints is important, but to truly understand people, we need to go beyond just acknowledging their opinions, and actively accept and value those opinions. This is something you cannot do if you only care about how "right" others are.

This may sound big and serious, but sharing and receiving opinions is just as important in small talk because it keeps conversations flowing and interesting. Too many people, however, shy away from sharing what they genuinely think, and they are just as unwilling to accept the opinions of others. They want to be polite and want others to like them, so they stick to safe topics and refrain from saying anything that could be vaguely seen as controversial. This is a mistake!

By freely sharing your opinions, especially on trivial topics, you contribute to engaging dialogue. Being proactive in offering opinions prevents conversations from becoming stagnant, and it sends a message that you are willing to be open and authentic. This invites others to do the same, and the result is a growing sense of trust and intimacy.

You may be one of those people who already has loads of strong opinions. Or you may be someone who is less sure about what they think and is not really in the habit of expressing themselves. If the latter sounds like you, then the challenge is to have the courage not only to know yourself, but also to *share* yourself.

Becoming an expert on oneself is key. The more you think about and share opinions, the more your brain becomes adept at forming and expressing them, leading to more engaging interactions. It goes without saying that whatever opinion you hold, try to express it with a balance of consideration and confidence.

To Enhance Your "Opinion Articulation," Practice the Opinion Speed Test

Challenge yourself to respond to these personal opinion questions within three seconds. The idea is to become more comfortable quickly expressing your opinion in the moment.

1. What's one of your favorite desserts?

2. What's your biggest pet peeve?

3. If you could only keep one book, what would it be?

4. What new technology would you like to see exist?

5. What's your favorite car?

6. What celebrity would make a good president?

7. What's the best place to visit in your town?

Of course, the exact questions given aren't important. Neither are the answers, for that matter. The point is to simply help you gauge your ability to articulate opinions quickly.

Could you answer the above comfortably and within three seconds? If not, then know that you may need to develop this skill and improve your capacity for spontaneous and effective conversations. You never need to be able to launch into a perfectly delivered twenty-minute TED talk. In fact, your answers don't need to be perfect or even true! But you should feel confident enough to answer without feeling awkward or put on the spot.

Sprinkle Your Opinions on Everything

Practice the habit of articulating your opinions on various topics. The irony is that people who have been taught to keep their opinions to themselves often find that they are out of practice when it comes to speaking their mind, and when they finally do so, they may express themselves in clumsy or unintended ways.

If this sounds like you, then challenge yourself to start small and add your personal opinions here and there. Initiate discussions of personal feelings and preferences. This doesn't mean veering into the deep-and-meaningfuls, but simply sharing your experiences and thoughts, such as your ideas about a favorite scene from a book or movie. Offer positive, playful, or complimentary remarks to others to foster engagement.

For example:

"That was a pretty interesting lecture, wasn't it? I definitely didn't expect that last part."

"Ooh, here comes the rain. I love it so much when it rains . . ."

"Those are amazing shoes, by the way. I like anything silver."

It's usually best to share opinions that are genuinely harmless and positive—say what you like or love, mention something you've noticed, or express things like interest, gratitude, or pleasant surprise at things in your shared environment. This is not to say that you should never share "negative" opinions or feelings—you absolutely can. If you're new to speaking up, however, and you're mostly trying to improve your small talk skills, keep things light. More weighty opinions can be saved for "medium" and "big" talk—here, personal disclosure can be a powerful tool for fostering trust and connection.

Use Hyperbole and Definitive Statements

A useful trick in small talk is to keep your opinions light and positive but express them in very colorful or even hyperbolic ways. This light-yet-colorful mode of expression takes a little practice but can be like sprinkling gold dust into a conversation. The trick is to use strong, even over-the-top language to express opinions and preferences in a way that is quite entertaining.

For example:

"These fitting rooms have the most flattering light in them. I don't know what magic lightbulbs they use, but I urgently need one in my bedroom!"

"Is there anything more delicious/grotesque than a greasy Philly cheesesteak sandwich from a food truck? If there is, I haven't found it yet."

"They have ___ here? This place wins. This place is my new favorite diner. I want to live here forever."

"That is the worst character on TV. I think he may give me high blood pressure."

"That was probably the most embarrassing moment of my life. I swear I could almost hear the tumbleweeds blowing by . . ."

What About Beliefs?

While opinions are portrayed as temporary subjective views that can be challenged, beliefs are more permanent subjective views—and we are a whole lot more resistant to changing them.

Belief is often rooted in cultural or personal faith, morality, and values. Shaped by individual experiences, knowledge, upbringing, and societal influences, beliefs can range from strong to weak and may evolve over time. Interactions with others and personal experiences can reinforce or change beliefs, which in turn can motivate or hinder behavior.

Beliefs make us who we are, but they also tend to make us shut out alternative perspectives. This hinders our social and personal growth and makes great conversation that little bit more challenging.

When engaging in small talk about beliefs, especially on sensitive topics like race or religion, it's important to approach the conversation with tact and consideration. Here are three tips on how to share your beliefs in small talk:

Listen to understand, not to come up with a counterargument.

A golden rule, and not just for small talk. *Actively listen to the other person*! Instead of immediately formulating your response, take the time to genuinely hear what they're saying. For instance, if they express an opinion on a political issue, just pause for a moment. Resist the urge to respond immediately with your own take. One excellent trick to cultivate your own ability to simply engage (versus argue) is to ask a question every time you're tempted to blurt out a counterargument. Stay curious.

Remember that you are not obliged to defend your beliefs. Don't be afraid to say, "I don't know."

Don't feel pressured to have all the answers at once. You never have to "defend" your beliefs or yourself. If you're unsure about a particular aspect of your beliefs or lack specific knowledge on a topic, it's perfectly fine to admit it. For example, if asked about a religious practice you're uncertain about, respond with, "I'm not entirely sure, but let me look into it and get back to you." This shows humility and a willingness to learn, which can foster a deeper conversation. There's nothing wrong with having no opinion or admitting that your current beliefs are a work in progress. There's nothing wrong with saying, "You know what, I'm not sure. I haven't figured that out yet."

Trust your personal experience.

Your lived experiences are valid and valuable, even in casual conversations. You can relax in that—and your relaxation will lead to easier, more enjoyable interactions. Trust in your own perspective, and don't let intimidation deter you from sharing your thoughts. For instance, if discussing a topic you're passionate about and which directly affects you, confidently and calmly express your own view. You don't need to convince anyone, apologize for your belief, or turn it into a game of tug-of-war. The more secure you are in that, the easier it will be for you to ask questions about *their* perspective and genuinely be willing to hear about it without feeling threatened.

Good conversation is always respectful and considerate, but that doesn't mean it has to be censored or boring! We all have opinions and beliefs, and we are entitled to them, but we also have the responsibility to express and share them well.

The HEFE Formula

HEFE is an acronym that will help you start conversations a little more easily. You focus on four main topic areas: hobbies, entertainment, food, and environment (that's referring to immediate surroundings, not things like climate change!).

Ask most socially anxious people and they will probably say that the beginnings of a conversation are the most challenging. The HEFE method offers a sense of control and predictability in those crucial first moments.

You can even use the acronym to prepare a few "canned" responses and comments ahead of time, so that they're ready to go in the heat of the moment.

It's not that being prepared in itself helps you be a better conversation partner; rather, it's the feeling of security and confidence that you gain from convincing yourself that you're prepared. It's this feeling of ease that allows you to engage more easily. The truth is that an awkward slence is no big deal and easy enough to manage in the moment; if you're socially anxious, however, you may allow a temporary lull to mean more than it should, and this can throw you off and color the rest of the interaction. Having a framework like HEFE in the bag is a little like having a comfort blanket—you don't *need* to be prepared in this way to have a good conversation, but knowing that you have it if needed will give you confidence.

The "environment" aspect of HEFE is especially helpful for people who are feeling anxious in social settings because it shifts the focus away from themselves. This shift is significant because social anxiety often stems from negative self-perceptions and concerns about how you will be judged by others. Self-consciousness almost always increases the more we monitor our own internal discomfort. Shifting attention outward, however, cuts down this anxiety and gets you actively engaged with what matters: the person in front of you and the interaction you're having with them here and now.

You can use HEFE to help you share information about yourself, or else keep attention on the other person so they can share information about themselves. The easiest way to get a conversation going from a cold start is to simply ask a question. For example:

Hobbies

"Are you doing anything outdoors this weekend? I always love hiking when the weather's this nice . . ."

"Did you watch the game last night? I'm a big fan myself."

"So how long have you been coming to salsa classes? Do you do any other type of dance?"

Try to avoid the very obvious "What do you do for fun?" questions since this can sometimes put people on the spot. After all, if someone asked you this question out of the blue, would you have a ready answer for them? It's a better idea to try to connect this question to something that is currently relevant. Consider context clues.

Entertainment

"I watched [big box office hit] last night at the movie theater. Weird film! Have you seen it?"

"Read any good books lately? I'm reading [title of book], but I'm not sure I like the author's style."

"Ooh, I love this song! Do you know [relevant band/group]?"

Again, you can see that this technique works best when connected to something happening at the moment—perhaps a song is playing on the radio in the background, or you spot them or someone else reading a book or something interesting in a newspaper or magazine.

Food

"Oh man, I would sell my soul for a good lasagna. What about you? What's your favorite food of all time?"

"I'm thinking of making fish for dinner tonight. Do you cook?"

"The only thing missing here is an ice cream stand, don't you think? What's your favorite flavor?"

Food is a topic that can get surprisingly deep surprisingly fast! Because food is a topic so close to many people's hearts, don't be surprised if food chat very quickly leads to all sorts of confessions, revelations, and plenty of strong opinions! It's prime small talk material.

Why Focusing on the Environment Helps

The final letter in the acronym is for environment, and it may be the most important one.

"Do you usually take this bus? Is it always this late?"

"This place actually used to be a Starbucks a few years ago. Do you live in the area?"

"Wow, it's busy today. Is there something special happening this weekend?"

According to Jenny Woo, creator of *52 Essential Conversations*, HEFE topics are easily accessible and low stress for everyone involved, reducing intimidation levels. This is especially true for topics that stem directly from the immediate environment. They don't require specialized knowledge and encourage sharing opinions, building better mutual understanding. When it comes to starting conversations, remind yourself that the beginning is actually the smallest, easiest part. The very second you start speaking and break the ice, the conversation has begun! Once you have that first rung in place, you have something to build on.

A: "The only thing missing here is an ice cream stand, don't you think? What's your favorite flavor?"

B: "Hmm, let me see. I don't know . . . I guess I like all the flavors?"

A: "No way, that's breaking the rules! You have to have one that you like more than all the others, right?"

B: "Yeah, okay, I guess I really love pistachio . . . but you can never get good pistachio ice cream around here."

A: "Yeah? Where *can* you get it?"

B: "Oh, that's easy—[place name] is the best, hands down. I think I had the best ice cream of my life there."

A: "I've heard of [ice cream place]. That's over in [area], right? By the arcade?"

B: "Yeah, that's it. I grew up just down the road, so maybe I'm biased!"

By constantly anchoring into simple, low-stakes topics and making reference to the environment, you can keep small talk starts easy and painless. Think of it this way: People who are friends are emotionally close because of what they share. That may be a shared history, a shared experience they went through together, shared opinions, shared jobs or lifestyles or hobbies, or even other people they know in common. When you meet a stranger, one of the quickest ways to establish rapport is to deliberately create this sense of a *shared* experience. And in any situation, two people are always going to be sharing something obvious . . . the environment around them.

They're waiting for the same bus. They're getting rained on by the same weather. They're hearing the same announcement over the speaker. Noticing these potential points of shared experience (even if they're tiny) gives you a little "in" and provides that first step for connecting to another person. It will almost always be the easiest and most comfortable entry into a conversation, and better yet, you won't need to memorize any rules or tricks. Just pay attention to what is happening in your shared environment, and see if you can formulate a question or response that will help you draw the other person in.

When you're feeling anxious and self-conscious, your attention narrows and tends to focus only on yourself. Consequently, it feels like there's absolutely nothing in the world you can think of to say. But if you relax, expand your awareness a little, and put your attention outside of yourself, you will suddenly realize that there are plenty of interesting conversation topics all around you. All you need to do is pick one and run with it.

Starting a conversation actually requires very little from you, and there are dozens of safe and comfortable topics to get you going. Sure, they can be pretty superficial, but think of them as just the spark that gets the fire going.

A great exercise to practice is to go about your daily life in public—in stores, on the street, in cafes and restaurants, at work, etc.—and practice paying attention to environmental cues that you could use to start up a conversation from scratch. You don't have to actually start the conversation, just practice becoming aware of potential threads in the environment and challenge yourself to think of ways you could use those cues. For example:

- You see a guy with a full sleeve of interesting tattoos. "Wow, nice ink. Did you get that whole thing done all at once?"
- You see someone buying five bunches of kale at the supermarket. "Wow, that's a lot of kale. I bet your mom is proud of you for eating all your veggies!"

- You see people in line to buy lottery tickets. "How much is the jackpot this time?"
- You see a woman walking an unusual dog. "Can I ask what breed of dog that is?"
- You see someone fiddling with a parking meter, looking confused. "Seems like you need a PhD in engineering to work these things, right?"
- You see a dad with three sunburnt kids at the beach. "It's such a hot day out today, isn't it?"
- You see a man reading a history magazine with a front-page story about World War II. "That looks interesting. Are you a big history fan?"

The more practice you get at noticing what is happening in your immediate environment, the more you'll realize that there are certain evergreen topics that always provide an entry into conversation. These include comments and observations about fashion trends, vacations, pets, kids, fad diets, mild run-ins with the law (like a parking ticket!), where you can get the best pizza, harmless but irrational fears, gossip about celebrities, how crazy world leaders are, how unfathomable men/women are, how nice/awful the weather is, how expensive things are, popular movies, seasonal stuff (Christmas, Halloween,

Valentine's), sports, how busy people are, how far away the weekend is, etc.

While you may be tempted to think of these topics as superficial and banal, they are actually worth their weight in gold. That's because they are "cheap" and easy, readily available, abundant, and almost guaranteed to help you ease into a comfortable conversation with minimal risk of awkwardness.

Knowing How to "Medium Talk"

If you play your cards right, you'll realize that small talk really doesn't last all that long—it's a *transitional* form of communication. It's meant as a kind of entrée and warm-up, and ironically, the more fully you engage with it, the more quickly you can move on to meatier conversation.

But wait! Before you head into the deep and meaningful conversations, be aware that there are many more shades and nuances between the first meeting and becoming best friends. These stages can be more complicated to manage than simply sparking up a little small talk.

Consider Ben, who actually finds small talk easy but struggles more with that vague, ill-defined state that happens afterward—that place where people are acquainted and have met but are not friends or even expecting to be. Ben comfortably sparks up new conversations with strangers and finds it easy to share, listen, and ask thoughtful questions. He is intelligent and has plenty to say on plenty of topics. He is also sincere in his intention to meet people, to form strong friendships, and to really connect.

And that's where the trouble starts . . .

This desire means that he immediately launches into deep and rather intense discussions. He gets excited about sharing his passions, quickly becoming carried away with a heated rant or soliloquy on his favorite topic. He sometimes blurts out things that are too personal, too controversial, or too intense. Though it feels like a good idea in the moment, he realizes after the fact that in his rush to force intimacy and closeness, he has actually created awkwardness. People pull back or "ghost" him, and he's left feeling a little embarrassed and overexposed. The problem is obvious: Ben does too much too fast, and it backfires. It's a little like turning up to a first date and proposing marriage after five minutes!

"Medium talk" refers to conversations that go beyond small talk but are not quite deep or meaningful enough to be considered significant. These conversations typically occur in social settings where people have limited connections and may never interact again. In medium talk, participants engage in slightly more substantive topics than the usual small talk, allowing for a brief moment of connection and potentially learning something new about each other.

It involves asking questions or discussing topics that prompt a bit more thought or introspection, moving beyond the surface level of polite exchanges. While medium talk may not lead to profound insights or lasting relationships, it can add some depth and interest to otherwise mundane interactions. Medium talk is essential—it's the key step between acquaintance and good friend, should that be a possibility, and it's a zone you must navigate with care and patience.

Now the bad news: medium talk is trickier than small talk. Small talk shows you're not an enemy, but medium talk suggests you could be a friend—big difference. It's about being both interesting and safe—and that can be a delicate balance to strike. While small talk is fine for quick interactions, medium talk is for longer chats in familiar but unintimate settings like work events or weddings. It's important to keep medium talk engaging without being controversial.

To avoid landing in awkward situations like Ben, take care to manage your intensity levels. It's a question of pacing. Avoid divisive topics and keep the conversation moderate—light but still enjoyable. Stick to mildly controversial topics that will stimulate more nuanced responses but won't lead to serious disagreements. This keeps the conversation interesting without causing tension.

Medium talk can also be transitional. If both parties are interested in eventually cultivating a friendship or relationship, then the task is to *gradually* ramp up intensity and closeness. The idea is that you slowly increase familiarity and closeness, giving the other person an opportunity each time to reciprocate each invitation to get that little bit closer.

Gradually, familiarity and trust grow. But if this delicate process is not done gradually, as in Ben's case, the effect can be extremely awkward and clumsy. Taking it slow is also a way to minimize any misunderstandings or potential clashes. If you stick to being moderate, you can always backpedal and save face if things don't work out.

This brings us to a big part of what makes medium talk so tricky: Medium talk can be transitional and lead to bigger things . . . but it doesn't necessarily have to. There are certain situations, dynamics, and people who will stay in the medium talk zone indefinitely. This includes:

- People you only meet infrequently, say once a year or so (distant relatives)
- People you don't necessarily like but need to maintain good relations with (work colleagues, in-laws, co-parents)
- People who are in your social sphere but not necessarily your friends (colleagues, spouses of close friends)
- People in positions of authority over you (teachers, mentors, bosses)
- People you will spend a lot of time with, but only for a defined period (those you meet during a conference, wedding, vacation or for a special work project)

One of the first things to do is to correctly discern whether the person you're speaking to falls into the "medium talk" category. Once you've made your introductions and engaged in a little small talk, you will find yourself having a slightly more substantial conversation. Think of pitching yourself somewhere in the middle—be mostly uncontroversial, but *slightly* interesting, as shown in the following graph:

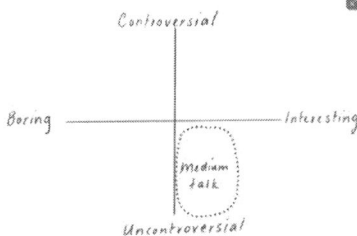

Controversial

Boring —————————————— Interesting

Medium
talk

Uncontroversial

The topic in this area, in practice, is lot of excellent talk falls into this boring side.

If, as time goes on, you have reason to believe that the connection can evolve and deepen, then you can try gradually increasing intimacy by being a little more controversial and personal. It's wise to assume, however, that initially, medium talk should stay medium. Don't be like Ben and take good rapport as permission to launch into being instant best friends! Instead, follow some of these medium talk rules to stay in that nice, happy medium zone:

Stay Relatable

In medium talk, the topics discussed should be accessible and meaningful to the average person. The goal is to initiate conversations that don't require extensive background knowledge or deep expertise. In a way, you're still on the same topics you might broach in small talk—you're just going a little deeper with it.

Most of us live inside our own social bubbles and can easily forget that our perspectives and attitudes are not necessarily the default for everyone. Be mindful of this and don't make any assumptions. Stick to classic topics that comfortably apply to most people in most circumstances.

Polarize—But Just a Little

Medium talk should introduce *some* level of polarization, meaning that the conversation can evoke differing opinions or preferences among participants. This helps in making the conversation more engaging and memorable.

But the big key here is that you are only introducing very small doses of contention and controversy purely to bring in a little depth. This may take the form of asking a very unexpected question or sharing a mildly unpopular opinion of your own. What counts as "mild"? Unfortunately, there can never be any rules about this since every social situation is unique. If you're unsure, test the waters with something that is only nominally controversial ("I secretly love pineapple on pizza") and go from there.

While polarization is encouraged, medium talk should steer clear of diving into topics that could lead to genuine heated controversies. Steer well clear of big gnarly topics likely to get people on the defensive. There *is* a small chance that you find your opinion perfectly mirrored in the other person, but if it isn't, it can be difficult to recover the conversation.

Remain Insightful

When you're talking to people you are not really familiar with, you may have very little idea about the way they communicate, their values, their perspectives, and their overall worldview. You cannot be sure of their background, their life goals, and all the things that matter to them. This is why it's best to start on a safe "home ground" rather than assume that they will understand or agree with a topic that you pick for your own convenience. Choose topics that are likely to be understood by anyone.

Despite being accessible and relatable, medium talk should still offer some level of insight or thoughtfulness. You want to start injecting a little of yourself into the mix and going beyond the normal, conventional themes and approaches. The goal is not to be as outlandish, intense, or sincere as possible, but rather just to gently introduce an unexpected perspective or to bring a little more energy into things.

Avoid Being Overly Intellectual or Complicated

Often, people try to hurry social interactions past the small and medium talk stage because they assume that "big talk" is more interesting, more intelligent, and more valuable. We may fear that the more superficial conversational levels are a little stupid or boring, or that they lack sophistication. One consequence of thinking this way is that we may be way too eager to launch into what we see as a worthy topic—something impressive or clever-sounding, or something that relates to our personal interests and values. Basically, our ego gets in the way.

Film director Woody Allen once asked seventeen-year-old supermodel Twiggy in an interview, "What is your view on serious matters? Who is your favorite philosopher?" The question was quite rightly seen as a poor attempt to embarrass Twiggy (which she managed to deflect) and not as a sincere attempt at interesting conversation.

The trouble with broaching serious intellectual topics is not that they are "too big" but rather that they tend to be about creating an impression of intelligence—often at the expense of the other person. Your goal should always be to connect. Forcing certain "highbrow" topics may merely alienate people, or worse, invite them into an ego-driven competition for who can say the most correct, clever-sounding thing.

Medium talk should strike a balance between depth and simplicity. It shouldn't delve too deeply into complex or highly intellectual subjects, and it shouldn't dig too deeply into minute details.

Summary:

- The best conversationalists don't hide their flaws; instead, they embrace them. Vulnerability is not an impediment to connection, but a prerequisite, so don't try to hide who you really are. People who express vulnerability and engage in open communication tend to have more positive social experiences and lower anxiety levels—they are confidently vulnerable. Embrace your weaknesses and insecurities as conversation material, and proactively acknowledge and use imperfections to your advantage. Use a little levity and self-deprecation.
- Opinions—yours and other people's—are intrinsically valuable, irrespective of what they are. Contrary to popular advice, it's wise to share your opinions and beliefs instead of being too generic and safe. The real skill is not to avoid entire topics or

refrain from sharing your opinion, but to be mindful of *how* you share.

- While opinions are portrayed as temporary subjective views that can be challenged, beliefs are more permanent subjective views—and we are a whole lot more resistant to changing them. Beliefs define us but can shut us off from new experiences. Be confident in yourself and realize that you don't have to defend or explain your beliefs; at the same time, "listen to understand" and be open-minded when encountering other people's beliefs.

- Use the HEFE formula (hobbies, entertainment, food, and environment) to quickly start a conversation. The "environment" aspect of HEFE is especially helpful because it shifts the focus away from us and onto the external world. Pay attention to what is happening in your shared environment and formulate a question/comment that will help you draw the other person in.

- "Medium talk" refers to conversations that go beyond small talk but are not quite deep or meaningful enough to be considered significant. It's trickier than small talk. Small talk shows you're not an enemy, but medium talk suggests you could be a friend—the key is to be *moderate* and *gradual*.

Chapter 3: The Nuts and Bolts of Conversation

In the last chapter, we turned a few common conversation misconceptions on their head:

Rather than hiding your flaws, try embracing them.

Rather than keeping quiet about your unique beliefs, opinions, and perspectives, share them calmly and confidently.

And rather than getting fixated on "good" or "bad" topics of conversation, be flexible enough to talk about *anything* (because you can if you do it in the right way).

The most important part of becoming a better communicator is understanding that how you say things matter more than what you say, and that your attitude and delivery are infinitely more influential than whether you agree with, understand, or like the person in front of you.

In this chapter we're going to take a deeper dive into the actual mechanics of conversation. If a good conversation were a machine, what kind of parts would it be made of? How would it function? What would it look like if it *didn't* function properly?

Four Key Elements of Every Conversation

Therapist Michelle Chalfant believes that a good place to start is to try to understand the purpose of conversation. For Chalfant (and many other therapists), **communication exists primarily to fulfill our innate need for belonging**. We talk so that we can connect. Therefore, it stands to reason that if we want to connect as well as possible, we need to get good at meeting people's needs to belong.

Now, in the next section, we'll see that there are a few other purposes behind communication (sharing data or solving problems, for example), but even these are indirect ways of meeting our deeper emotional needs—i.e., the need to be seen and heard, respected, included, and validated, as well as the need to belong and have one's contributions accepted.

Keeping this ultimate, deeper human need in mind at all times (yes, even when having the most superficial conversations!), we can now consider four key elements that make most conversations, big and small: We talk to ask, inform, include, or propose.

What's great about sticking to just these four elements is that it takes the pressure off. If you successfully include just these four elements, your conversation will feel balanced and engaging.

You don't need to worry about anything else, like *entertaining*, *lecturing*, *convincing*, *complimenting*, or *charming* the other person. When you're in the middle of a conversation, your anxiety can sometimes make it feel like the spotlight is on you and the clock is ticking. You may feel like you're supposed to say something witty, clever, amusing, or extra interesting—and say it fast. You don't! If you're stumped, just include one of these elements and go from there.

Asking

To master the art of making easy small talk, leverage the first element of conversation: asking. This involves posing low-pressure, straightforward questions that aren't overly personal, allowing the other person to feel at ease.

Licensed clinical psychologist Aimee Daramus recommends inquiries about music preferences, TV shows, or professional backgrounds, as these topics typically invite a relaxed response. In social settings, questions about how people know each other or their experiences at an event can also initiate conversations.

Are they the most thrilling topics in the world? Of course not. But that's precisely why they're valuable—there is an almost non-existent risk of intimidating, alienating, or offending people with any of these topics. The key to effectively use this element is to steer clear of yes-or-no queries (closed questions), and instead focus on using questions to encourage people to expand and elaborate.

Chalfant suggests using questions as an opportunity to seek recommendations, especially if the other person seems hesitant to share personal details. By framing your inquiry with a brief context, such as needing advice on buying kitchenware or a suggestion on a good show to watch, you prompt the other person to offer their insights and recommendations, facilitating a more dynamic exchange. Not only do they feel like their perspective and contribution is valued, but you'll also get things flowing without putting anyone on the spot.

Informing

This includes sharing interesting titbits about yourself, as well as offering your opinions, perspectives, and beliefs. Dr. Daramus suggests sharing experiences related to your profession or hobbies, and leading with anecdotes that invite follow-up questions. For example, a mechanic might share a humorous lesson he learned while working on a car, while a teacher could recount a memorable and unexpected classroom experience. Keeping these anecdotes short and a little mysterious will invite others to pitch in with their opinions, stories, or questions—and just like that the conversation begins to flow.

Sharing personal stories not only facilitates conversation but also alleviates the pressure of discussing unfamiliar topics—for you and for them. If you tend to feel shy or struggle with spontaneity, consider preparing little anecdotes or memories in advance. These could include fun childhood memories or recent discoveries about yourself. Additionally, consider bringing a homemade dish to gatherings, allowing you to share the story behind your creation and sparking conversation. You can also discuss your current TV interests and inquire about others' viewing preferences.

In business, people are encouraged to come up with a neat "elevator pitch," which is a brief explanation of who they are and what they do professionally. It can be a good idea to create your own informal elevator pitch for unfamiliar social situations.

You don't have to heavily script anything. Just be prepared to briefly explain who you are in an engaging way that fits the occasion. For example, if you're heading to a big wedding, take a few moments to rehearse a quick elevator speech that tells people who you are and how you're connected to the bride/groom, and maybe a few anecdotes about how you traveled to the venue or a cute story about how you know the couple.

Including

Social anxiety and shyness can make us hyperfocus on our own contributions to conversations (or lack thereof!). It can also mean we get hung up on how we appear to others. But according to Dr. Daramus, one underrated social skill is to notice when *someone else* seems quiet but displays signs of wanting to contribute, such as starting to speak or appearing engaged. In such situations, deliberately inviting their opinion can make a conversation feel so much more natural and balanced.

Two things happen when you choose to deliberately include others:

1. You immediately shift your focus from internal to external—i.e., from your own feelings of discomfort or awkwardness onto other people and their experience. This takes the spotlight off you and lowers your self-consciousness.
2. You demonstrate empathy, kindness, and consideration. People like those who are witty and charming, but they like those who are kind and considerate a whole lot more!

If you notice someone standing alone at a gathering, approach them with a relatable comment or a brief anecdote without making the interaction about yourself. For example, share a moment when you felt isolated at a party and allow them to share their thoughts in return (remember the power of leading with vulnerability?). Once they open up, expressing understanding or empathy can further strengthen the connection, making conversation more natural and comfortable.

Proactively trying to include others in this way completely changes your frame of reference—you are no longer an anxious outsider, wondering about how to impress anyone, but rather an active, comfortable participant in the social situation. The big secret is that people who are "popular" and comfortably social tend to do this naturally—they are so charming and appealing precisely because they are not heavily focused on themselves and how they appear.

Worrying how you come across to others is a way to give them too much power; it's a way that we may mentally exclude ourselves and assume that we don't belong. But the moment you switch your focus and get curious about how you can make others feel like they belong, you'll find that you feel far more generous, more relaxed, and more at home in social interactions. It's a revelation: Not only do you belong in a social situation, but your presence may even improve it!

Including others in conversation doesn't always have to be serious. Offering compliments also falls under this category, as does listening attentively and being genuinely curious about the value that others bring to the table. Whether it's praising someone's vibe or admiring decorations at a party, giving a genuine compliment not only makes others feel amazing, but it makes *you* feel great, too.

Proposing

Proposing simply means moving the conversation forward somehow. You may have noticed that even great conversations eventually lose steam or flag a little. Nothing lasts forever! Proposing something different is a way that you can actively "steer" things in a different direction. For example:

- You propose playing a game or grabbing another drink to keep the interaction lively and engaging.
- You suggest a "scene change"—going for a walk or moving to a new location to carry on the discussion somewhere else.
- You gently steer things away from tricky or uncomfortable topics when you notice them coming up.
- You suggest a new topic so that you can take things a little deeper/further, or else step back and have a break if things have gotten too intense.
- You could even combine proposing and including by drawing attention to someone else in the conversation and asking for their input if they've been quiet for a while.

If you're someone who doesn't find socializing and small talk easy, you may notice that a conversation is starting to lose momentum, and panic. You worry that you'll be left with nothing to say, or perhaps you start wondering whether they find you or the conversation boring. But the truth is that all conversations have a lifespan and a flow, and it's okay for an interaction to pass its peak and start winding down. Instead of allowing this observation to worry you, take it as a cue to propose a new direction/topic/activity instead.

One final word: Don't be afraid to "propose" the end of a conversation. There's nothing wrong with noticing that the interaction is coming to an end. Often, the dislike of small talk comes from feeling trapped in conversations that never end and having to keep coming up with new things to say long after enthusiasm has died.

Give yourself permission to gracefully and politely exit the conversation. Not only does this show a certain self-confidence on your part, but it may actually spare you from genuinely awkward moments later on when both parties clearly want out but don't know how to say goodbye. Brevity, as they say, is the soul of wit. Keep it short and sweet!

Understanding Conversation Types

Charles Duhigg is a communications expert and bestselling author of *Supercommunicators: How to Unlock the Secret Language of Connection*. Duhigg claims that, contrary to popular belief, being a great conversationalist isn't necessarily tied to personality traits like charisma or extroversion.

Duhigg's research indicates that *anyone* can develop strong communication skills if only they're willing to understand and apply the dynamics of conversation. It will be no surprise to you that the big secret behind "supercommunication" is to actively demonstrate genuine interest in connecting with others. This is the main insight we can take from Duhigg's work: **Supercommunicators understand conversation types**.

Why do people communicate in the first place? What's the point?

The obvious answer to this is: it depends. We communicate for all sorts of reasons. And that means that there are as many different types of conversation as there are reasons for communicating. Some might say that every single conversation is completely unique. Because supercommunicators understand this principle, they also understand that it's their job to master the rules of the game, so to speak.

Understanding the various modes of conversation is essential for mastering the way we connect, and it helps us build authentic, enjoyable relationships with others—even if those "relationships" are only fleeting moments of small talk with strangers!

By recognizing these patterns and developing skills to navigate them, we can engage in conversations that help our intentions align with their intentions. The result is that everything "clicks"—we feel seen and heard, problems are solved, frictions eased, new insights gained, and we feel more meaningfully connected to one another.

Right now, try to recall the last three conversations you had, even if they were brief or superficial. Now ask yourself, what purpose did that conversation serve? Why did it exist, and did it fulfill its purpose? Why or why not?

Thinking in terms of function and purpose may feel a little counterintuitive in some ways, but it may open your eyes to a whole new world of understanding. Whether exchanging information, sharing personal experiences, or addressing relational dynamics, understanding the deeper meaning behind every conversation gives you a secret superpower.

Let's begin by understanding the three broad types of conversations (i.e., the three different purposes that conversations tend to serve). Of course, there are some that serve more than one purpose, and some that may be very unique and specific to particular people in a particular environment. Nevertheless, almost all human interactions can be categorized as one of the following:

Informational/Practical Conversations

The informational mode of conversation primarily involves exchanging data, often for practical purposes, tasks, or goals. This mode is characterized by a lack of intense emotion and is focused on external topics. Examples include asking for directions, seeking opinions on a work-related issue, discussing a contract, or even passing the salt at the dinner table. While informational conversations are usually practical, it doesn't mean that they are completely devoid of emotion or that they don't create rapport. On the contrary, a well-flowing practical conversation can foster a sense of connection and belonging, especially when discussing shared interests or hobbies, or when working on a problem together.

The key point about this kind of conversation is that it revolves around *external* events and ideas. The ultimate purpose is external to both people having the conversation. It's not about delving deeply into personal emotions or relationships. It's not about analysis or abstract conjecture. In their earlier stages, many conversations may naturally fall into this mode, driven by a desire to sound knowledgeable and find common ground. There may be a shared point of reference that people talk about, and this external topic acts like a proxy or go-between between the people conversing.

It would be a mistake to think that this type of conversation is somehow inferior. The informational mode may well be perceived as lacking depth or excitement, but the world would be an overly intense and confusing place were it not possible to have concrete, practical conversations! Though the patterns are not set in stone, overall, more men than women tend to default to this conversation style, and a more practical engagement style may be preferred by people of certain ages, personality types, or backgrounds.

Tip: When engaging in the informational mode of conversation, prioritize clarity and brevity to effectively exchange information. Keep the discussion focused on practical matters and tasks at hand while recognizing the value of shared interests or hobbies. Think in concrete terms (when, where, what, how) and keep your focus on the external environment, preferably on what is happening right now.

Personal/Emotional Conversations

The personal/emotional mode of conversation delves into deeper, more intimate aspects of our lives, fostering connections and a sense of belonging. Just like the informational mode, the purpose is also to share information—but in this case the information is human information, and the emphasis is not so much on the information itself but on the feelings of connection created by sharing it.

Unlike the informational mode, which focuses primarily on external topics, this mode revolves around sharing *internal* experiences like emotions, perspective, and feelings. It's often characterized by a relaxed, safe atmosphere, typically occurring with trusted friends or in sympathetic environments like support groups.

In this mode, individuals open up about their joys, sorrows, and challenges, seeking empathy, understanding, and camaraderie. Examples include discussing job loss, caregiving responsibilities, exciting new experiences, or intimate relationships. As listeners, there's a natural inclination to comfort or advise those who share vulnerable stories, and receptivity and empathy are essential in fostering deeper connections. Emotional conversations *can* be light—for example, expressing a fond childhood memory or an inconsequential "secret" you have—but it always creates a feeling of affinity and warmth.

Both speakers and listeners may encounter discomfort in this mode, however. This mode of conversing is not necessarily superior or always appropriate, and even when it is, it doesn't mean there aren't risks. Speakers may feel vulnerable or disappointed if their stories aren't received as expected, while listeners may struggle with uncertainty or eagerness to change the topic. It can be tricky to keep intensity levels matched. Despite these challenges, embracing the personal/emotional mode allows for more meaningful connections—in fact, it's often the only way we can access that kind of connection.

Tip: Practice active listening and empathy to validate the speaker's emotions and experiences, reciprocating vulnerability by sharing one's own feelings authentically and offering support without judgment. As you listen, imagine that there are two streams of information: the facts of what you're being told, but underneath that, the emotional content attached to those facts. In a more personal conversation, train yourself to listen to and respond to the emotional content first.

Relational Conversations

The relational mode of conversation involves addressing aspects of the relationship or conversational dynamic itself. This is a kind of meta-communication, where the purpose is to talk about the relationship itself and reflexively work on communication as a tool to help both achieve their desired ends. In fact, many conversations of this type focus on *purpose* itself and how a mismatch in respective purpose may be causing misunderstanding or conflict. This book is, in effect, a kind of relational conversation between the author and the reader.

Of all three conversation types, this may be the least common, but when used may have the greatest impact overall on relationship quality. Whether someone approaches these interactions with excitement or dread, they are essential any time you need to directly appraise the effectiveness of communication and "get on the same page." Relational conversations require a high degree of relational intelligence to navigate effectively—and like the other forms, there is a time and a place for them.

In its simplest form, the relational mode involves steering attention toward the **dynamic**, rather than to emotions about the dynamic or to specific concrete details. For example, a couple may have an argument about the dishwasher on Friday. During this argument, tempers flare and both act out from their own perspectives and emotions.

On Saturday, things have cooled off a little, and one of them asks, "Can we talk about what happened yesterday?" If during the ensuing conversation someone gets angry or distracted by the details of which dishes were and were not placed in the dishwasher, someone else could ignore this and instead refocus on the dynamic: "I've noticed that you often criticize me for things that you yourself do. Then we end up in arguments like this. Can we talk about better ways to give me feedback? I don't want to feel so defensive all the time."

Relational conversations often occur during transitions, such as negotiating business deals or addressing changes in personal relationships. They can also arise spontaneously to address feedback, conflict, appreciation, or withheld feelings, and you may have noticed that this kind of reflexive analysis is common in talk therapy.

Knowing when and how to shift into relational mode is a valuable skill—and it doesn't need to be deep and serious, either. Consider the example of a first date that isn't going very well. The conversation is fizzling and energy is low, so you say something like, "Hey, is it just me or is the vibe feeling a little off here?" This instantly takes the conversation to a new level and, done with a warm smile and a genuine attitude of respect and curiosity, is likely to help both of you navigate the situation so much better.

Tip: Navigate relational conversations with finesse by directly addressing aspects of the relationship or conversational dynamic. The trick is to guide interactions toward a greater sense of *shared purpose and connection*. It may feel a little cheesy in the moment, but don't be afraid to directly express needs, boundaries, or desires, and ask others to do the same.

The Art of Asking Good Questions

Emily has always been an anxious person, and socializing tends to bring out the worst of her anxiety. All the advice she is given tells her that a surefire way to "win friends and influence people" is to ask plenty of questions. People who talk too much about themselves, we're told, are boring and come across as a little self-absorbed, so it's better to show interest in the other person and ask them all about *their* life.

So far, so good. When Emily applies this strategy, however, it doesn't quite work the way she wants it to. She can't put her finger on why, but even she can tell that conversations feel somehow forced. She even begins to find them a little formal and joyless, and she doesn't understand why—aren't people supposed to like talking about themselves? Isn't it good to ask questions?

The truth is that asking a question is *not* a universally good move. That's because questions can be many things and serve many different functions. There are no good or bad questions per se, but rather it's about *when* a question is asked, and *why* and *how*.

Unfortunately, Emily defaulted to asking questions whenever she felt anxious—which was often. This meant she asked too many rapid-fire questions, none of which really connected to one another or to the ideas and concepts unfolding in the conversation. Her questions were not tailored and didn't emerge naturally out of the conversation—and as a result they felt artificial, almost like a job interview or interrogation.

Used well, questions can bring depth and closeness, but the wrong questions at the wrong time can actually create more distance, misunderstanding, and awkwardness.

So, what distinguishes a good question from a bad one?

There are two answers to that. A "bad" question is:

1. Simply poorly formulated, or
2. Well-formulated, but asked at the wrong time, in the wrong way, etc.

An ideal question is **a genuine expression of curiosity and interest** that respectfully invites the other person to share something of themselves. It moves the conversation along and creates depth, interest, and clarity. Questions that are poorly formulated, on the other hand, just don't do any of this. They're often not questions at all, but rather statements disguised as questions, for example.

- "You don't have a clue, do you?" (There is no comfortable answer here because it's not really a question.)
- "So, what part of my presentation did you like the best?" (It's an assumption that you liked any of it!)

- "That's crazy, right?" (This is more like an order: "Say you agree with me about this.")

"Questions" like this may have their place, but they're just not capable of conveying the kind of respectful curiosity that benefits conversations. Be mindful of the way you might be using questions to conceal statements—it's a sneaky habit that many of us have!

On the other hand, a question may fail to create rapport and connection simply because it's used in the wrong way. To understand this better, we need to have a clear understanding of the many different functions that questions can serve, and then make sure that we're using the right question for the job—almost like selecting the best tool from a toolkit.

Function 1: To Help You Understand Better

Use **follow-up questions** to help you gain a deeper understanding of what you're being told (and, in the process, convey to the other person that you want to understand). This simply means that you ask a series of questions that build on one another, as well as build on the previous answer. For example:

A: "Where did you go on your vacation to California?"

B: "We spent a day at the San Diego Zoo!"

A: "Oh, cool. I love the zoo. What's your favorite animal there?"

B: "Well, it'll sound silly, but I really like the meerkat enclosure. I could watch them for hours."

A: "Oh yeah, I remember them. Are the kids also meerkat fans?"

B: "Actually . . ."

As you can see, each of these questions builds on the answer to the previous one. There are three questions in a row here, but they don't feel intrusive since they are seamlessly embedded into the flow of things. Compare this with the following interaction (which is characteristic of Emily's question style):

A: "Where did you go on your vacation to California?"

B: "We spent a day at the San Diego Zoo!"

A: "Have you been to California before?"

B: "No, first time. Well, my wife went once when she was younger."

A: "How long was your vacation?"

In this example, there are also three questions in a row, but these questions are likely to come across as far more interrogatory. That's because they don't lead on from the answers, they don't develop, and they don't flow. The answers about visiting the zoo or the wife having visited once before are not really acknowledged or followed up on—Person A just dives in with the next, unrelated question. These rapid-fire and disconnected questions can create a feeling of not really being listened to, or of being interrogated.

If a person uses this question style exclusively, people may start to feel that they are being asked to share parts of themselves while the interrogator conveniently shares nothing in return. This can create a subtle feeling of power imbalance or lopsidedness. If you are asking people to reveal a little of themselves and their lives, it's a common courtesy to reveal yourself to the same extent so people don't feel as though they're being put in the spotlight and examined!

WHEN NOT TO USE: Follow-up questions are almost always a good idea, but try to avoid too many in a row—three is a good limit. Also avoid endless follow-up questions on details that are truly trivial, or you risk coming across as pedantic and boring. Notice the topics that people seem to be especially animated and emotional about and target your questions there.

Function 2: To Gather Specific Information

Use **direct questions** if you're looking for straightforward answers or you're seeking specific information. If you need basic facts or want to clarify a few details, keep your questions "closed" and to the point:

"What happened at the party?"

"When did you arrive at the office?"

"Where are the car keys?"

WHEN NOT TO USE: When someone is expressing their emotions. For example, if someone sadly tells you their dog died, respond to their sadness and acknowledge it ("I'm sorry. How are you feeling?") rather than probe for facts and details ("What did it die of?").

Function 3: To Demonstrate Listening and Empathy

Use **reflective questions** to show that you are listening to the other person and care about the emotional content of what they're saying. While direct questions ask for plain facts and data, reflective questions are not designed to extract information at all—but rather to reflect and validate that information so that the person feels "heard."

"Do you think you're feeling a bit frustrated by the whole situation?" (gently putting a label on a feeling or experience and inviting the other person to share how they feel).

"Why do you think he said what he did?" (less focus on the fact of what was said, and more focus on how it was perceived).

"What do you think you're most worried about?" (in response to a broad statement about fears for the future—a recognition of that emotional content and invitation to further).

WHEN NOT TO USE: Empathy and listening are always valuable, but in certain circumstances they should not take precedence. If your interaction is brief, professional, practical, or focused on a narrow set of problems and solutions, then avoid questions that probe emotions—ironically, you may come across as a poor listener!

Function 4: To Summarize and Confirm

Ask **summary questions** to recap the information provided by the respondent, giving them a chance to review and clarify their answers. This question type also serves a dual function of showing that you're listening and paying attention.

Let's say you have a five-minute conversation where someone shares a few statements about the pros and cons of a new car they're planning on getting. The conversation is open-ended, but eventually you say, "So, all in all it sounds like you're considering a red full-size luxury car for commuting and weekend trips?"

This question serves two purposes: It brings this particular thread to a neat close and signals that you are "wrapping things up," but it also demonstrates to the other person that you have not only been listening, but understanding and synthesizing everything you've heard. Like the previous question type, this can help the other person feel validated. In conflict situations or misunderstandings, a question of this type also works to signal to the other person that you intend to be fair and reasonable, and that you are interested in understanding their side of the story. Simply asking, "Have I got that right?" is an incredibly effective way to signal your willingness to cooperate.

"Let me make sure I understand. You're saying that the issue arose due to miscommunication between departments, correct?"

WHEN NOT TO USE: Summary questions are best used when there is actually something to summarize! Avoid them for very short and superficial interactions.

Function 5: To Fill Space

Use **impertinent questions** as a kind of buffer or conversational lubricant. These questions are unrelated to the main subject but can ease tension, provide a break, or gather indirect insights. Many people think that this style of question has less value because it is superficial or even a kind of distraction—but that's exactly where its power lies.

These are the kinds of questions you might ask casually while waiting for a bus or in a doctor's office. People may not be in the mood to discuss what is most relevant at that moment (how annoying it is for buses to be late, their embarrassing medical conditions), so non-pertinent questions can come to the rescue. They keep interactions warm and friendly, keep up the flow of conversation, and build relaxed rapport—all without going too deep.

"How long have you worked at this company?"

"What's your favorite hobby outside of work?"

"Do you have any vacation plans coming up?"

WHEN NOT TO USE: Avoid asking a space-filling kind of question when you're in a conversation that's already flowing well. If you interrupt a good flow with a random superficial topic change, the other person may feel cut short. For instance, suddenly asking a question about the weather when the person is excitedly sharing something personal with you may be felt as a rupture or lack of interest.

Function 6: To Detect Deception or Inconsistencies

Finally, you can use so-called **control questions** when you already know the answer but you want to gauge the truthfulness, attention, or behavior of the respondent:

"How did it go in the performance review with Pamela today?" (You know how it went; you want to see what they have to say about it.)

"What did you do with the missing file?" (You know they lost it, but you want to see how they're going to explain themselves.)

"Did you attend the training session last week?" (You know they did, but you want to start a conversation about this training session.)

Sometimes these kinds of questions can be used during conflict to establish and confirm certain details or to find agreement on a shared set of facts. ("So the file was already lost when you went to look for it on Tuesday?")

WHEN NOT TO USE: This is not your typical small talk territory! Avoid asking questions like a detective uncovering "what really happened" in conversations that are not meant to be serious. The very worst response to humor and lightheartedness is to take things too seriously.

As you can see, what works in one context may completely flop in another context. The next time you're in a conversation of any kind, pay attention to the kind of questions you're being asked, and be curious about the function they may be serving.

Why is the person asking? Are they genuinely looking for data/information, or are they trying to be friendly and show an interest in you? Are they trying to fill space and pass the time, or are they trying to deliberately gather more information so they can better comprehend what you're saying?

In the same way, think about what kind of questions best match the situation you're in and the person in front of you. When Emily learned to do this, she realized that most of her awkward encounters came down to a mismatch in question style. For example, someone might be sharing a personal anecdote and she'd ask too many questions about the details, or else grill them about the facts. On the other hand, she might lead with plenty of kind, concerned questions intending to show empathy, when the other person merely wanted to quickly exchange some useful information.

A good rule of thumb is to quickly appraise the overall purpose of your conversation, no matter how brief it may be—are you trying to create a connection, solve a problem, or pass the time pleasantly? Decide what you're doing first, and then choose your questions accordingly.

Summary:

- Communication exists primarily to fulfill our innate need for belonging, but there are different ways it can meet this need. When we speak, we can do one of four broad tasks: ask, inform, include, or propose. If you successfully include just these four elements, your conversation will feel balanced and engaging without too much pressure. Focus on low-stakes, relaxed questions that encourage people to expand and elaborate.
- Informing includes sharing interesting titbits about yourself, opinions, perspectives, beliefs, and anecdotes, whereas including means deliberately drawing other people into the interaction

and will make you feel more comfortable and proactive. Proposing means moving the conversation forward somehow or suggesting a new direction/topic/activity—including ending the conversation.

- There are three main types of conversation according to their purpose: informational/practical (concrete, external events), personal/emotional (all about feelings and inner experience), and relational (reflecting on the relationship dynamic itself). Understand which one you're in and adjust accordingly. Being a supercommunicator isn't necessarily about innate charisma or extroversion, but understanding the nature and function of conversation types.

- Similarly, the kind of questions you ask depends on what you're trying to achieve. Functions include helping improve your understanding, gathering more data, showing empathy and compassion, summarizing and confirming, filling space and creating a pleasant distraction, or occasionally detecting inconsistencies or deceptions (this last one is rare). There are no good or bad questions per se, but rather it's about *when* a question is asked, and *why* and *how*. Pay attention to question type and function.

Hopefully you're convinced that there is, contrary to popular advice, a place in everyday conversation for your "flaws," your opinions, and your personal beliefs. In fact, with practice you may start to see these things not as impediments to good conversation but as necessary ingredients—a set of superpowers, even. Likewise, there is no "right" thing to say or best question to ask—only what is appropriate for that person, in that conversation, at that time and place.

The big skill behind cultivating conversational flow is the ability to know exactly when to share an opinion and when to ask for one, when to push and when to pull, when to stay factual and when to delve a little into emotions and personal perspectives. In this chapter we'll look a little more closely at the idea of a conversational "sweet spot"—that is, that perfectly flowing state where conversation is varied and lively.

Maintain Conversational Flow with FOOFAAE

In the moment, a well-flowing conversation can feel almost magical, and it's hard to pinpoint exactly why things are "clicking" so well. Luckily, we have a few tools to help us deliberately create this feeling of flow. One of these tools is the "FOOFAAE" acronym. It offers us a structured approach for making sure that we are including plenty of **varied elements** in our conversation. These elements include: feelings, observations, opinions, facts, action statements, autobiographical elements, and events.

Exceptional conversationalists seamlessly integrate these categories, while poor conversationalists may rely too heavily on a few. Again, we see the same principle emerge: It's not that any one element is good or bad; rather, what matters is the fluidity with which we are able to move between different elements.

Using the acronym is easy. The next time you're in a conversation, realize that at any moment you are at liberty to choose the kind of contribution you make, and in doing so, steer the tone and direction of that conversation. Let's say that you're in a small talk situation with someone and chatting about their dog. Using FOOFAAE, you can choose between the following:

FEELING: I absolutely love your dog.

OBSERVATION: You have such a well-behaved dog.

OPINION: I think pugs are the best kind of small dog breed.

FACT: I was reading that pugs are usually ...

ACTION STATEMENT: I want to adopt a dog like that.

AUTOBIOGRAPHICAL: My brother has a pug too ...

EVENT: Did you hear Frank just adopted a dog last month?

In the above example, the speaker has shared their own opinions, observations, etc. You can also use this framework, however, to guide the questions you ask or shape the comment you make about *their* opinions, feelings, and so on.

Let's take a look at another example where you may focus more on the other person. Let's say you meet a stranger at a party and they start telling you how they've just sold their house and will be hopefully moving into a new one the following month.

FEELING: Wow, I'm guessing you're feeling pretty relieved to be done with the whole process!

OBSERVATION: Two months? That seems like a quick turnaround.

OPINION: How did you find your realtor, by the way?

FACT: Apparently the average house price in that area has gone up twenty percent in the last year.

ACTION STATEMENT: So, what's next for you guys?

AUTOBIOGRAPHICAL: Is this your first big house move?

EVENT: I heard they're putting new streetlamps on that road.

Feeling comments are simply anything to do with your preferences, feelings, expectations, hopes, desires, etc. **Observations** are typically more objective statements than **opinions**. **Facts** are information or knowledge. **Action statements** are any comments that involve an action (including a potential or past action). **Autobiographical** comments involve personal details, stories, etc. **Events** are past, present, or future occurrences.

Now, to the person listening, all of the above statements will feel like "small talk," but they are actually quite different from one another and liable to produce different responses and reactions. Each category serves a distinct purpose, from expressing preferences to sharing knowledge or initiating actions.

There are a few ways to apply this acronym in your own life. First, use it to help you become more aware of your own conversational tendencies, habits, and biases. You may not even know that you have a habit of, for example, always making comments that refer to events and never sharing opinions or feelings. Once you notice this, however, you give yourself the chance to mix things up a bit and bring more flow and balance to the kind of contributions you make in social interactions.

Another way to use this acronym is as a kind of conversational lifeboat. When you feel stumped for something to say or can sense that energy and momentum are being lost, quickly consult the acronym and see what elements may be missing. Many conversations stall because there is too narrow a focus on too small a thread of conversation. For example, you may both get trapped in sharing facts and details back and forth and find things quickly becoming dull. Realizing this, you can add a breath of fresh air by switching to opinions, feelings, or action statements. Subtly switching tack this way can help shift stuck conversations and drive things along a bit more proactively.

A third way to use FOOFAAE is to help you tailor your comments to fit the unique person you're talking to. Being in the "sweet spot" is a question of deep engagement with *this* person and *this* topic right now in *this* moment. When your comments are strategic and specific, you quickly allow yourself to engage more deeply, and conversations become juicier and more authentic. For example, if you have reason to believe that the interaction is best kept quite superficial, you may deliberately rely more on comments about facts and events. If you're in a work context, for example, this will subtly convey a sense of professionalism and composure that will bring a sense of rapport and harmony to the interaction.

Or you may be talking to a fellow parent at the school gates one day and realize that it's more appropriate to add comments that are autobiographical or action based. Your small talk may revolve around the kids, the activities they're doing, and what might happen in the future. In still a third example (let's say, a quick chat with a person you've just met on an online dating site), sticking too much to facts, events, or actions may feel a little impersonal. Here, more comments focusing on feelings and opinions may be required to create that sense of flow.

One final way to use FOOFAAE is as a kind of diagnostic tool. In other words, when a conversation isn't working or flowing well, you can quickly take a step back and become curious about why—could it have something to do with the type of comment or statement you've just made? For example, let's say you're chatting with a new acquaintance and the conversation is flowing well. Suddenly, though, there's a small rupture, an awkward silence, and a few moments of discomfort.

You ask yourself, what happened right before this awkwardness? What kind of statement seemed to precede the rupture? Taking it further, can you notice any ongoing patterns with this person specifically or with people in general? You may not be able to "diagnose" a problem using FOOFAAE alone, but you may spot subtle reasons for an interaction taking a turn. For example, an awkward silence may consistently follow a statement or comment that is about feelings or opinions. Noticing this, you decide to stick to other kinds of statements instead and observe that things flow better that way. Congratulations! You've now learned something important about this person and how they like to communicate, or about the shared context and expectations about the kind of interaction you can have.

Those who are naturally "good with people" can make these subtle shifts and adjustments almost unconsciously and intuitively. Because they are able to quickly switch the kind of contribution they make, they maintain a state of flow and seldom find themselves in awkward spots or outright conflict. There is nothing magical about this skill—it's simply the ability to remain aware of what you're doing and the effect it's having and knowing how to change in real time to achieve a different effect.

Tune into how the person in front of you wants to communicate. Some people love a nerdy fact-based conversation about hobbies or current events or whatever is happening right there in the moment. Some people want to talk about feelings. Some people want to reminisce about the past, while others are energized by making plans and preparing for events that are yet to happen. Some people love to keep things abstract and intellectual; others want to keep it concrete and straightforward.

Conversational flow does not require that both people are the same, or that they think and communicate the same. It only requires a kind of *flexibility* and willingness to be in the moment. If the person you're speaking to looks like they're getting bored, you don't have to change the topic of conversation—experiment with changing the perspective on that conversation.

For example, you're talking to someone who doesn't care about sports, and you notice that introducing this topic immediately creates a kind of mini rupture. No problem! Stay on the topic of sports but change up the *way* you speak about it. For example, instead of boring the other person with the game you watched last night (facts, events), you can shift to talking about why you *loved* it so much (feelings, opinions) or how it's a part of your Sunday tradition at home (autobiographical).

Thinking this way allows you to uncover new angles on an old topic and center the connection and flow rather than dwell too much on the details of the topic itself. Being flexible, curious, and willing to flow with the other person means you could soon find yourself having a fascinating dialogue about the psychology of the sports-lover, the importance of baseball to the American national identity, or the incredible nuances of the big business behind the game. Handled correctly, you may find that your conversation with this sports-hating person is the most interesting conversation you've ever had about sports!

It's important to recognize that establishing a smooth conversation flow may take time and practice—even if you've mastered a trick like the FOOFAAE acronym. A perfectly smooth flow is seldom guaranteed, especially when talking with people you're unfamiliar with. That's why it's worth managing expectations and being patient with yourself and with others. Always keep an open, receptive mindset.

The person in front of you has something interesting to teach you and share with you— be curious about what that could be and adjust your dialogue in whatever way necessary to help you uncover that gem.

Upgrade Your Words

"So, how are you doing?"

"Yeah, I'm okay. You?"

"Fine."

"Nice weather we're having."

"It's great!"

Have you ever had a conversation with someone where you weren't even sure what you both said? Words were definitely spoken, but all of them seemed . . . meaningless. Generic and lifeless language is a big risk when it comes to small talk, but when used deliberately, words possess extraordinary power.

The right words are capable of shaping perceptions, influencing decisions, and forging connections. They serve as the building blocks of our interactions, whether we're engaging in casual banter or navigating critical moments like job interviews or romantic encounters. Words matter!

Consider the impact of a well-chosen word in conversation. In moments where first impressions matter, a single word uttered at the right time can dramatically alter the trajectory of an interaction. Whether it's infusing humor, evoking emotion, or sparking curiosity, your choice of language holds the potential to captivate and intrigue (or for that matter, offend, confuse, or alienate).

As we've said in many different ways, small talk doesn't have to mean superficial, boring, or unintelligent talk. Take, for example, the difference between describing someone's breath as merely "bad" versus "gross" or likening it to "dog food" or even "fish pie that expired in 1923." Each variation adds layers of imagery and personality, transforming a mundane observation into a memorable anecdote.

In general, words serve as the currency of small talk, lubricating the wheels of social interaction and fostering camaraderie. In casual settings, such as networking events, parties, or coffee shop encounters, the art of small talk relies heavily on our ability to wield language with finesse. If you only have a few minutes and a few words to make an impression, why not choose those words wisely?

Here are a few practical ways to upgrade your words in casual conversation:

Elevate Mundane Descriptions with Vivid Language

Transform ordinary descriptions into captivating narratives by infusing them with colorful language and analogies. Rather than settling for mundane descriptions like "nice," use descriptive words like "delightful" or "satisfying" or "the best thing that happened all morning." By using inherently interesting words, vivid imagery, and unexpected adjectives, you add a little jolt of electricity into the interaction. It makes the other person stop and pay attention.

Experiment with Wordplay and Creativity

Break free from conventional language patterns by adding wordplay and creativity. Sprinkle your conversations with unexpected twists and turns, experimenting with different combinations of words and phrases—this kind of lighthearted fun is contagious and sends the message that you are relaxed and confident. For instance, instead of saying, "I need to do my laundry," you could say, "Time to tame the laundry monster!" This playful twist adds an element of fun and creativity to an otherwise mundane chore. Suddenly, there is something brand new and unique about the interaction—something for the other person to grab hold of and run with.

Harness the Power of Labels and Categorization

Tap into people's tendency to label and categorize by giving unique names to individuals, actions, intentions, or situations. Adding labels this way adds depth, triggering emotions and memories in the people you're talking with and creating a mini "in-group."

Whether you call your daily stair-climbing routine "corporate aerobics," or affectionately nickname your daughter the "Squirrel Whisperer," these labels make ordinary experiences so much more interesting and memorable. Naturally, while you're doing this, you're also subtly expressing your own opinions and perspectives, but in a gentle, indirect way.

Enhance Conversations with Contrasts

One great way to add color and dimension is to consider using contrast. By playing around with opposing elements in your statements, you create dynamic and interesting angles that stand out against the mundane. It's all about being just a little unexpected. Whether you're comparing experiences, observations, or preferences, contrasts naturally draw people in and make your dialogue more compelling.

For example, instead of saying, "I've always had dogs growing up," add a contrast: "I've always had dogs growing up. Cats are just too high end for me, I'm afraid!"

Or consider: "My kids mean the world to me. Of course, I still want to strangle them every day ..."

"So, I signed up for a marathon at the end of this year. I've, uh, yet to locate my running shoes, but I feel I'm making progress."

You can contrast anything: reality versus expectation, your actions versus someone else's, or normal versus extreme experiences. Each contrast adds depth to your conversation and makes it more specific—which makes it more real and meaningful.

Remember that when it comes to your flaws and weaknesses, it doesn't matter what they are—it only matters what your attitude is toward them and how you choose to reveal that part of yourself to others. Likewise, when it comes to opinions and beliefs, no topics are off-limits, because it's not what you think or believe, but rather *how you express* yourself that matters.

Politics, money, religion, and sex are all topics that can be safely and successfully broached if done in the right way. By using "upgraded" language and vivid imagery, and by expressing yourself honestly and respectfully, you can talk about anything to anyone:

- "Things were really tight this month money-wise. I keep telling my cat to get a job and contribute to the bills, but his English isn't very good, and he never listens" (here, humor is used to add color and levity).
- "Well, if there *is* a God, he probably loves eavesdropping on conversations like this

one, right?" (being playful and relaxed, rather than needing to make any serious theological claims!).

- "Is John gay? Well, he's had about fourteen thousand girlfriends, so I'm inclined to say no . . ." (here, a delicate topic is handled with obvious hyperbole. The exaggeration actually helps you avoid saying something potentially offensive).

- "Oh, I totally see where you're coming from with this issue. Personally, I'm more on the conservative side of that continuum, but there's a lot of overlap, isn't there?" (earnestly and comfortably acknowledging political difference, but choosing to focus on similarity instead).

On the other hand, you could talk about the most generic and conventional topic in the world and still cause offense and awkwardness if you do so in a clumsy or boring way. Even a person talking about the weather can cause plenty of awkwardness and bad feelings if they do it in a hostile and negative way!

It's Also About What You DON'T Say

When Leah started a new job at a retirement home, part of her was dreading having to interact with all the elderly people. She hated small talk and envisioned having to endure hours and hours of tedious chat about "old people topics." She considered herself a very vibrant, driven person with a wide range of interests, and wasn't looking forward to politely sitting through boring conversations about people's grandkids or their health problems.

Leah was in for a huge shock. Once she started speaking with the retirement home residents, she quickly had to reassess her assumptions. Every person there was fascinating. All her preconceptions were blown out of the water, and she found that not only were conversations not boring and predictable, but that in many cases, *she* felt like the boring one!

When was the last time you sincerely learned something new from someone? When last did you have a conversation where you thought, "Wow, that's interesting. I honestly never knew that before"?

Chances are, it's been a while. If most of us are honest, we may hold certain assumptions and preconceptions about other people—all those ideas and beliefs that make us say, "I hate small talk." These biases are not easy to admit, but they include thoughts around other people simply not being that interesting.

Have you ever secretly (or not so secretly) felt that everyone else was just a little bit more stupid than yourself? That their opinions and perspectives were predictable, and their tastes conventional? These are very normal biases we all have—it's easy to imagine that our own inner worlds are rich and unique and special, while other people are so much less interesting, right?

Consequently, we may treat other people as foregone conclusions. We may make snap judgments about who they are and what they'll say or do, and never listen for long enough to realize that our stereotypes about them are very wrong.

Being introverted, shy, or socially anxious means we often avoid going deep with other people. That means that we only know our *own* minds, and perhaps the minds of a very select few people who are close to us. Everyone else, because we don't know them, starts to look two dimensional. Without realizing it, we may find that we increasingly don't see them as people at all, but supporting characters, a uniform mass of what we collectively call "other people."

But every single other person is a unique individual, just like you. They have an inner world that is as rich and complex as yours, and they are as dearly attached to their experiences and perspectives as you are to your own. All this sounds obvious, but it's a point we may forget if we're out of practice socially. Because we don't actively engage with other people as they are, we start to make assumptions about what they think and feel and who they are.

Those who succeed socially have a genuine, sincere belief that other people are valuable. That engaging with them has value in its own right. That it's always possible to learn something from someone, no matter who they are. Ask yourself honestly if you are holding on to negative biases about other people that could be leading you to underestimate them. Do you have any assumptions about what "people" are like?

Below are a few simple tricks you can try to gently shift your attitude in this area. These techniques may seem very simple, but prepare to be surprised at how effective they can be.

1. Wait three beats after someone finishes speaking before you speak.

When you're in a conversation and someone else finishes what they are saying, wait three beats (count one . . . two . . . three . . .) before you start responding. Three beats might not seem like much until you're actually in the moment—and then it seems like ages! Be aware that the idea is not to have your response ready and then patiently wait three beats before you let it out of your mouth. Rather, wait three full beats before you begin mentally putting together your response.

Deliberately pausing in this way creates space. That space is where the other person can continue to unfold and reveal themselves. But it's also space for you to properly absorb what you've heard and process it before rushing in to say something else. Often, people are in a hurry to speak over one another. They hear what they think is the gist of what's being said, and before the other person is actually finished saying it, they have already launched into their response.

A great thing to remember is to "listen to understand, not to respond." Really take your time in the moment without thinking about all the things you want to say in return. You may find that the other person actually wasn't finished fully expressing themselves. You may find that they're actually not saying what you thought they were.

Most of us are so used to being interrupted or talked over that that three-beat pause is more than enough to convey genuine listening and attention. Assume that people have something interesting to say, and then give them the space to say it. They'll love you for it!

2. Strive for a 3:1 ratio of questions to statements.

Here's another cheesy but one hundred percent accurate truism: You have two ears and one mouth, so listen twice as much as you speak. In fact, make the ratio even more in favor of listening by offering roughly three times as many questions as you do statements. An effective approach to try is maintaining a 3:1 ratio of questions to statements—that's three questions for every statement made.

Person A: "I had a great weekend; I went hiking in the mountains."

Person B: "How was the weather up there?"

Person A: "Actually, it was way colder than we thought it would be . . ."

Person B: "Oh, really? That sucks. Who did you go with?"

Person A: "My family, or I should say my mom and dad and two of my brothers."

Person B: "You have more than one brother . . .?"

Person A: "Haha, I do! I've got three brothers and a sister. We're a pretty big family."

Person B: "So that's five of you all together. I think it's so great having that many siblings. I was an only child, and I always wished I had an older brother or sister to look after me!"

In this example, there are three questions from Person B (note as well that they are thoughtful follow-up questions that quickly get the conversation moving). Only after these three questions does Person B share a statement of their own about themselves.

You don't need to strictly stick to one question at a time, however. You can ask two or maybe even three at a time, or sandwich your questions and comments together—what's important is that the overall ratio stays roughly the same:

Person A: "I had a great weekend; I went hiking in the mountains."

Person B: "How was the weather up there? Did you go alone?"

Person A: "No, I went with my family. We stayed two nights in our cabin, which is usually pretty warm, but this time it was below freezing . . ."

Person B: "Oh, wow! I'm such a city girl I could never do that, honestly. But I suppose the cabin is set up with everything you need? Do you have, like, a proper shower?"

Person A: "Nope! It's pretty basic. Have you ever been out hiking overnight?"

Person B: "No, never. I'd be afraid a bear would eat me or something . . ."

It's important to note that this ratio isn't meant to be a rigid rule, but rather an exercise in fostering an attitude for receptivity and open-mindedness. Let go of where you think the conversation should go and just relax a little, seeing where it is right now. One thing you may notice as well is that by being more generous with your attention, by listening more, and by asking more questions, you actually enjoy conversations more. In other words, letting people speak is not some grand sacrifice!

Perhaps you've been conditioned to think that conversations are only interesting or worthwhile if you're talking, or if the topic relates directly to you. Practicing the 3:1 rule will convince you that relaxing and sharing the flow has a certain magic to it—somehow, *everyone* feels more heard.

Focus on crafting open-ended questions that don't elicit simple "yes" or "no" responses, and seek answers that you don't already know. Notice where people get especially excited, and pay attention to the topics that seem to grab them. Those are the topics you want to ask about!

3: Don't lecture or preach.

When you're explaining yourself, making an argument, or telling an anecdote, aim for a maximum of three supporting sentences and one conclusion. Think of it as an argument with a maximum of three premises and one conclusion—"I think X because of this reason and this other reason and this third reason." Then *stop talking* and let other people take "the floor."

Person A: "We were lucky to get cheap tickets that time. Do you like going to concerts?"

Person B: "Oh, I love them! The energy, the vibe . . . I love the whole atmosphere. Actually, what I think I like most is that it's such a great way to spend quality time with friends. These days everyone's lives are so busy, and we seldom get a whole evening just to hang out with each other like we did back in college, you know?"

Person B's response above is just about the maximum length for a small or medium talk conversation. You can see the three "premises" quite clearly. Person B isn't getting carried away and talking too much; they're answering the question, explaining their reasoning, and leaving plenty of threads for Person A to pick up on.

Think of it as speaking in bullet points. Of course, if you're having a more serious, in-depth conversation with someone you already know well ("big talk"), then you can elaborate on your points in more detail. For small talk, however, keep things bite-sized—more like a listicle than *War and Peace*. If you're a chronic over-talker, keep reminding yourself that you don't have to say everything at once. Take a deep breath, trust that the other person has heard you, and let it go.

One Simple Story

How good are you at telling stories? What about jokes or funny anecdotes? Have you ever found yourself repeating a fascinating or hilarious story to someone else, only to watch it flop when *you* tell it?

Don't worry—being a good storyteller is hard! Nevertheless, you can get better at it with just a little practice. While some people naturally excel at storytelling, anyone can improve by learning to frame their real-life experiences as stories, then practicing how they deliver these stories. Yes, we're talking about preparation again.

Skilled storytellers understand that stories work when they are *emotionally engaging . . .* and they intentionally shape their encounters with this in mind. A big part of becoming a better storyteller is simply treating all experiences as potential stories to share later. Yes, even if you don't think you live a very interesting life, I can guarantee that you have plenty of good story material to work with. There's a common misconception that only grand adventures or remarkable discoveries make for good stories. Even everyday experiences, however, can be engaging if told with a twist and presented well.

Confident people excel at storytelling not because their lives are genuinely more interesting or entertaining; rather, it's because they believe their lives are worth sharing. It's in their attitude. Everyone possesses interesting stories; the trick is knowing how to draw them out, find their best bits, then frame them in just the right way.

In the same way that comedians refine their routines through repetition, crafting stories involves honing them over time—either by yourself in preparation, or by telling the story to others. Each retelling helps trim away dull parts and solidifies the memory of the story. In time, the story may improve, but you are also getting more confident every time you tell it—

and that confidence itself makes the story that much better.

Conversations shouldn't feel like performances. Sharing stories should stem from a genuine desire to communicate your life, not from a need to impress or entertain others. Otherwise, your storytelling may come across as insincere or self-serving. Transforming an interesting experience into a story, however, does require a little bit of effort. With practice, nearly anyone can become a proficient storyteller. Using the steps given below, start with just one good story and build your collection as you go.

Three Steps to a Great Story

There are about a million different ways to tell a story, but if you break things down, you will see that every good story consists of just three essential components. Even without being aware of it, all of us expect the following three components for a psychologically satisfying story:

Status Quo: ONCE UPON A TIME . . . This establishes the current situation or belief, presenting it as a fact without any conflict or change.

Conflict: BUT THEN . . . Something disrupts or challenges the status quo, introducing tension or a problem that needs to be addressed.

Resolution: AND SO . . . The conflict is resolved, providing an answer to the problem or question raised by the conflict and leading to a better outcome.

Status quo, conflict, resolution. These are the basic building blocks of *any* story. Unfortunately, we often overlook the conflict part, which prevents our audience from fully engaging with our narrative.

Let's see how much more engaging the "status quos" become when we add the conflict in general storytelling:

Status quo: The itsy-bitsy spider climbed up the waterspout.

Conflict: Down came the rain and washed the spider out.

Resolution: Out came the sun and dried up all the rain, and the itsy-bitsy spider climbed up the spout again. You go, Itsy! (Yes, we're on a first-name basis. We go way back.)

Leave any of these elements out and you may find your audience thinking, "So what?"

Let's apply the three-step storytelling structure to telling a personal anecdote in conversation.

Status quo: Begin by setting the scene and establishing the current situation or background of the anecdote. For example, "Last weekend, I decided to try cooking a new recipe for dinner."

Conflict: Introduce the conflict or challenge that arises in the story, creating tension or a problem to be resolved. This could be an unexpected turn of events or a complication that arises. For instance, "But halfway through the recipe, I realized I was missing a key ingredient—tomatoes!"

Resolution: Finally, share how the conflict is resolved or how the situation is resolved, leading to a conclusion or outcome. This could involve problem-solving, improvisation, or a surprising twist. For example, "Instead of panicking, I got creative and substituted the tomatoes with roasted red peppers. It was a disaster. Long story short, we ordered pizza!"

Granted, this isn't going to win any Pulitzer Prizes, but it *is* a sound anecdote with a solid structure. Once you are comfortable with this three-part structure, you can begin to embellish the framework to adapt and adjust stories as necessary. Jokes, for example, are just stories where the resolution is told in a humorous or unexpected way. The same story could be told in an entirely different way, such as a personal story that shows a little of your vulnerable side. No matter what, though, the three components are always there.

A few more tips:

Have a Good Hook

To keep a good flow, say something like, "That reminds me of the time . . ." and then lead into your story. Naturally, you want to make sure that your story does really connect in some meaningful way. It can be a good idea to deliver your story in three distinct parts, but leave a little mystery between each beat, so that people are encouraged to literally ask, "So what happened next?" This can be a great way to build engagement and can be a lot of fun.

Keep It Short

Being nervous can mean we sometimes say way more than we need to. Perhaps we start a story far too early or carry on long after the resolution has been reached, including loads of irrelevant detail along the way. Deliberately practice only including the most important bits, and cut the rest. If you find yourself listening to someone else's long and rambling story (hey, it happens), then it can be a fun exercise to challenge yourself to listen for the three parts and imagine how you could tell the same story but in just fifteen seconds or less.

Be Vivid and Include Details

Just because you're being brief, however, it doesn't mean you can't express yourself and be colorful. Try including just one or two vivid details that will bring your story to life. You can have fun adding other elements, too—use facial expressions or mimic someone else's voice or body language to "act out" various parts of the story. Stand-up comedians will often work for months on a single joke, playing around with timing, delivery, and exact word choice. You can do the same by focusing on just a few key details that add interest, polishing them till they shine.

Study Natural Storytellers . . . And Take Notes

Speaking of comedians, they can be great to watch closely. Ask yourself *why* a certain story or joke works. You can sometimes see how a comic's routine may even change over the months and years—pay attention to these changes and what they're doing to make things funny and engaging. Sometimes, all it takes is a pause in the right place, a lifted eyebrow, a certain gesture, or a particular turn

149

of phrase to turn a so-so joke into something truly hysterical.

Good storytelling is an art, and you can learn a lot about it by watching the masters work. You can also observe inspiring public speakers or dissect interviews with charismatic celebrities. Note everything they do and see if you can begin to incorporate some of it into your own storytelling.

Don't Forget this Secret Ingredient

People listen to stories because they want to follow the narrative arc of a character. The only reason they want to do that is because they *care* about that character. They are emotionally invested. Any good story has to matter emotionally to people, or they simply won't care. You don't have to make your stories heavy-handed or over-the-top; simply make sure there is an emotional core holding the whole thing together.

Maybe your story is amusing because of how embarrassing it must have been. Or maybe it's a story of a "near miss" that captures people's attention because of how shocking, unusual, or lucky it was. Maybe your story is good to hear because it's about something warm and fuzzy, a satisfying tale of justice, reward, or the thrill of a mystery solved. Even *Itsy-Bitsy*

Spider is at its core an inspiring story about hope and resilience!

When you're practicing and preparing your stories and anecdotes, bear this in mind and make sure that you have a clear idea of what you want your audience to **feel**. Then tailor everything in the story toward this end—that includes your nonverbal expression and body language.

Summary:

- The big skill behind social success is cultivating conversational flow (i.e., knowing how to introduce and change topics on the fly).
- Use FOOFAAE to help you maintain variability in topics, and include observations, opinions, facts, action statements, autobiographical elements, and events. No single topic is better than another. What matters is the fluidity with which we are able to shift topics. Stay balanced and tailor your approach. Tune into how the person in front of you wants to communicate.
- Upgrade your words and use colorful, unexpected, expressive language instead of being predictable and generic. Be vivid and creative, and experiment with exaggeration, analogy, and contrast.

- Don't make assumptions about others or treat them as "foregone conclusions." Instead, be willing to be surprised by people. Wait three beats after someone finishes speaking before you speak, and strive for a 3:1 ratio of questions to answers in conversations. Genuinely listen to them and refrain from lecturing and preaching. Be willing to find out exactly what you can learn from every new person you meet. Don't rush, and "listen to understand, not to respond."
- To tell great stories, you need just three steps: an intro to establish a baseline, a surprising event/conflict, and an emotionally satisfying resolution. Your everyday experiences can be engaging if told with a twist and presented well. Keep stories short and to the point, and always include some emotional core to keep people invested.

In our final chapter, we'll be exploring all those ways that, despite our best efforts, conversations can flop. Whether it's a lack of empathy (or the wrong kind of empathy), some kind of imbalance, a mismatch in contributions or styles, or a weird little moment of misunderstanding, conversations can and do go wrong sometimes. Being a skilled conversationalist simply requires that we know how to handle ourselves when things don't go to plan . . .

The Empathy Formula

Zara has always felt like an outsider. Having been bullied as a child, as an adult she finds it extremely difficult to make friends, to assert herself, and to chat comfortably with people on the spur of the moment. One day, Zara is surprised to hear from a close friend that when they first met her, they actually found her "a little cold." The friend explained that Zara initially seemed a bit mean and judgmental. Zara is shocked by this admission—she always assumed that people were judging *her*.

How do we explain this?

One of the unfortunate realities of social anxiety is just how much it can remove us from the present moment, from ourselves, and from other people. When we are anxious and preoccupied with our own self-conscious feelings, we turn inward and lose connection with the outside world. For some people, that can mean coming across as uncertain, unconfident, and submissive. But for other people, their shyness can actually make them appear to others as aloof and even a little arrogant. This may not seem fair, but there is truth in the observation made by Zara's friend: When we are preoccupied with our own anxieties, we *actually are less empathetic.*

Because Zara was spending so much mental energy and attention on trying to survive and navigate stressful social situations, there wasn't much mental energy left over to spend on other people. The result was that she often failed to ask people questions about themselves, failed to give praise or compliments, failed to be warm and friendly, and failed to really listen to what other people were saying to her.

For example, during a Zoom call with fellow students on her university course, Zara remembers how intensely she stared at her own face on the screen, scanning for anything potentially embarrassing, monitoring how she might appear, and trying to "act natural." At the end of the meeting, however, Zara could recall nothing of what went on. She couldn't remember who else was in the meeting, what they looked like, what they said, or what the lesson was even about. From Zara's point of view, she was anxious and hyper focused on her own stress throughout the entire meeting. But from the other students' point of view, all they saw was someone who was *not engaged*.

The ability to empathize is crucial in navigating conversations of all kinds. It's a skill that requires emotional literacy and self-awareness—and it also requires that we're sufficiently outside our own heads!

The reason we begin this chapter with Zara's story is to emphasize that a lack of empathy is not always about being a deliberately mean, uncaring, or unkind person—in fact, we most often fail to empathize properly simply because we're preoccupied with our own drama and are just being inconsiderate. Everyone likes to think that they're an above-average driver and that they have especially good taste, and it's the same with empathy; nobody likes to imagine that they are not being empathetic.

The truth, however, is that all of us have the ability to forget about others, to center ourselves, or to make lazy assumptions that serve us but potentially damage our connection to others. One of the biggest reasons that conversations fail is a rupture caused by a lack of empathy. Many of the issues we've already explored (such as not understanding the type of conversation the other person wants to have) are basically about empathy and the willingness to imagine the world from a perspective other than our own.

Very simply, empathy involves understanding the experiences, perceptions, and feelings of another person. There are two ways that conversations can go bad due to a lack of empathy:

1. The other person makes an attempt to elicit your empathy, but you fail to respond (as in Zara's case).
2. You respond with empathy, but you do so in a clumsy or inappropriate way.

If you believe you may experience the first issue, then your challenge will be to externalize your attention enough onto others and the surrounding environment so that you can notice when other people are making a bid for your compassion. Simply get into the habit of asking yourself, in every interaction, how someone else might be feeling and how you might acknowledge, reflect, and validate that feeling. It could be as easy as saying something like, "Wow, you got one hundred percent on the test—you must be so proud!"

The second issue is a question of knowing exactly how to respond empathetically. For example, a colleague at work may subtly reveal a personal problem to you. How should you respond? There are actually *three* types of empathy: cognitive, emotional, and compassionate. While empathy is always valuable, being truly empathetic means understanding how best to show that you care.

Cognitive Empathy: This involves recognizing and understanding another person's emotional state through conscious, rational means, also known as "perspective-taking." As an example, consider an expert psychiatrist who specializes in depression. As they listen to a new patient talk about their feelings, they certainly understand what they're hearing and have an excellent grasp on what depression is—perhaps better than anyone. The psychiatrist, however, may never have experienced depression themselves, and while hearing their depressed patient speak, they may not personally feel any sadness themselves, or identify with that feeling.

We can imagine that this form of empathy is a little like seeing someone stuck deep in a hole, but we ourselves remain outside it, standing on the edge and looking in. Cognitive empathy is having an intellectual understanding and comprehension of someone else's experience, and this can be valuable in workplace scenarios, problem-solving, or professional situations.

Emotional Empathy: Emotional empathy is the ability to share in the feelings of others and recognize them on a more visceral, personal level. Whereas cognitive empathy is the ability to "know" what someone else is experiencing, emotional empathy is more the ability to feel into the experience of someone else, even if we are not having that experience ourselves. To return to our example, a close friend may reveal to you that they're feeling depressed and hopeless, and on hearing them, you can't help but feel awful on their behalf. You find yourself tearing up a little; you are not depressed yourself, but you have emotional empathy for their position.

This kind of ability to feel someone else's perspective for yourself is a little like seeing someone is in a deep hole, and actually getting in there with them. It's crucial in close relationships with friends, family members, or partners. It's also a non-negotiable ingredient for caring professions, or for mediation and peacekeeping.

Compassionate Empathy: This is considered the ideal form of empathy. It involves recognizing and feeling for a person's situation, but without feeling overwhelmed by it. This kind of empathy is the best of both worlds—we are able to feel what others feel, but not to the extent that we cannot help, guide, or support them. Compassionate empathy is kind and accepting, but also action-oriented.

It's analogous to seeing a person in a hole, getting down in there with them, but bringing a ladder with you and showing them how you can both use the ladder to climb out of the hole. This kind of empathy is effective in any relationship and is characterized by thoughtfulness, presence, and responses that focus on practically solving problems.

It's useful to really understand the difference between these types of empathy, since a lack or mismatch of empathy is often at the root of poor rapport in a conversation. Either one person is expecting more empathy than they're receiving, or else the *type* of empathy they're receiving is not quite right. Occasionally, someone may show too much empathy, but realistically this is a rare problem!

How to Use Empathetic Statements

It's important to realize that empathy is not something you feel. Rather, it's a message that you communicate to someone else, and it's primarily for their benefit. **Empathy is something you do.** Good intentions will simply not be enough—we have to carefully consider how we are showing our concern and compassion, and make sure that the message is tailored so that other people can genuinely receive it.

Empathetic statements convey understanding, validation, and support for the other person's feelings. They differ from sympathetic responses in that empathy involves truly understanding and connecting with the other person's emotions, while sympathy may involve just feeling sorry for them without fully grasping their experience.

Sometimes, people carelessly offer what they think is an adequate empathetic response, but really it is little more than paying lip service to cultural or social expectations. If you've ever been on the receiving end of this kind of "empathy," you will already know how hollow it can feel. We need to consistently remind ourselves that an empathetic response is not one that makes *us* feel warm and fuzzy and virtuous—rather, it's a response that stems from considering the other person, their perspective, and their needs.

Let's take a closer look at some less-than-ideal empathetic responses, consider why they don't work, and explore a few more effective alternatives.

- "I'm sure it's not as bad as you say. Just email your boss, and I'm sure he'll understand."
- "Don't be silly. You have nothing to feel guilty about."
- "Come on, I know you can handle this."

These responses all do one thing: invalidate. When we observe a person's emotional reaction but try to minimize it, deny it, or explain it away, we actually undermine their experience, even if our intention is to cheer them up or convince them the problem isn't so bad. Instead, try:

- "Wow, that sounds so stressful for you."
- "It makes sense that this would make you feel guilty."

161

- "I can see you're filled with doubts. I get it."

Take a look at the additional statements below and see if you can spot why they don't convey all that much empathy:

- "You poor thing, I can only imagine. I felt exactly the same when it happened to me."
- "You need to get out of the house. Take up running. There's no better therapy, believe me."
- "It might not feel like it, but there's a reason for everything. I just know it."

The problem with these responses is that they put too much focus on the speaker's experience, opinions, and perspective, and assume that it must be the same for the other person. It's human nature to want to share our wisdom and find commonalities between others' experiences and our own, but when we make ourselves the main point of reference, we're not really being empathetic at all. Instead try statements that put the other person front and center:

- "Tell me more. What happened?"
- "Is there anything you can do right now to try to take your mind off things? Something you enjoy?"

- "It sounds like you're having a hard time making sense of it all."

Other things to try to avoid include confusing pity for compassion, giving advice and platitudes, and rushing in to soothe and reassure when the other person merely wants to share how they feel and know that you've heard them.

An extremely useful formula:

[Reflect their experience by labeling their emotion and link it to a reason] +

[Expression of feeling] +

[Thoughtful question, suggestion, or offer of help].

Look closely and you'll see that this neatly includes all three types of empathy (cognitive, emotional, and compassionate). For example, if your work colleague told you about a personal issue they were struggling with, you could reply:

"Oh, wow, it sounds like you've been really overwhelmed [emotion label] because of everything you're having to take care of right now [reason]. I'm really so sorry that you've had to deal with this [expression of feeling]. I'm not sure what I can do to help, but I am here if you want to talk about it after work sometime [offer of help]."

Another example:

"I'm not surprised you feel like this. I'm sure the news came as such a shock [emotion label and reason—notice how the language validates the emotion as it names it]. I really feel for you [expression of feeling]. How are you managing with the kids at the moment [thoughtful question]?"

Give-and-Take—How to Have a Balanced Conversation

It's common today to see human variation in terms of extroversion or introversion—those who are comfortable being social versus those who aren't. We imagine that a gregarious extrovert is a good conversationalist, and a shy and retiring type must be a good listener, for example.

But if you've ever met a confident loudmouth who never let anyone get a word in edgewise, or else a timid wallflower who somehow never seemed to take any responsibility for keeping the conversation going, then you'll know that there's more to sociability than introversion or extroversion. In this section, we're going to take a slightly different approach and instead divide people up into "givers" and "takers."

In conversations, "givers" and "takers" refer to different approaches that people adopt when engaging with others.

Givers: They view conversations as a series of invitations. Givers are inclined to ask questions, show interest, and offer opportunities for their conversation partners to share. What they give to the other person is energy, attention, and opportunity. They create conversational "affordances," providing openings for the other person to contribute. Givers, however, may feel resentful if their efforts are not reciprocated, as they perceive conversations as mutual exchanges.

Takers: Takers see conversations as a series of declarations. They are more inclined to make statements, share their own thoughts, and take the spotlight. They take the available energy, attention, and opportunity and run with it. Takers can be valuable in keeping conversations flowing, as they contribute without waiting for explicit invitations. They may, however, sometimes dominate the conversation, leaving little room for others to participate.

Now, don't imagine that givers are better than takers! Rather, it's a question of how the two dynamics play out with one another. When two givers meet, the conversation flows well, just as it does when two takers meet. On the other hand, trouble can happen when a giver meets a taker. The giver gives, and the taker takes. The giver feels exhausted and resentful ("When do I get a chance to talk about me? How rude!"), while the taker either enjoys themselves and doesn't notice ("They must find me fascinating!"), or else gets bored or irritated ("Why does this person keep asking me questions? Is this an interview?").

Each of us has the potential to be either a taker or a giver, and we may adopt different roles depending on who we find ourselves talking to and in what context. Both approaches have their strengths and weaknesses. Givers facilitate engagement and mutual sharing, while takers keep conversations lively and dynamic. The key is finding a **balance** between giving and taking, offering and accepting conversational affordances. This involves being aware of opportunities to contribute and being receptive to others' contributions. It requires that we pay enough attention to notice who is giving and taking, and how we might adapt to make a conversation a little more harmonious.

Consider this example. At a party a group of four people assembles and starts talking. One of the people starts things off by asking how they all know the party's host. Because there are four people, it's not really clear who should answer this question first, so there's a little awkward fumbling. You see, there are three givers here—and each of them wants to "give" the limelight to someone else. The result is a conversation that doesn't really get going until the fourth person, a taker, simply decides to jump in and start talking.

This works well for a while, as the taker takes center stage and shares one amusing anecdote after another. But eventually, they get tired of being in the limelight and start to wonder why others aren't jumping in to share some of the conversational burden. The givers, too, are feeling a little annoyed, since their politeness and courtesy does not seem to have been reciprocated—the taker just talks and talks and never asks them to contribute.

Now, this might make for an awkward conversation or, if prolonged enough, a full conflict or misunderstanding. It's not anyone's "fault." The disharmony could be resolved either by the givers being proactive and taking the lead now and then, or by the taker shutting up for a few minutes to ask other people for their contribution. You see, neither introversion nor extroversion are good or bad; when your disposition is preventing you from engaging dynamically, however, it can be a problem, whatever your disposition happens to be.

Refusing to take the spotlight is not always generous, polite, or empathetic. Endless questions and deflections back to the other person can eventually be felt as avoidance or shirking your responsibility to carry your part of the conversation. At the same time, takers are often enjoying their own experience of the conversation to such an extent that they forget that other people are a part of it too—in other words, they take *too much* responsibility for where the conversation is going.

"Affordances" and Conversational Doorknobs

Psychologists and communication experts have identified what they call affordances. In general terms, an affordance is something in your environment that allows you to do something, like a doorknob (which by its existence allows you to open a door). Conversational affordances or doorknobs act in the same way—they allow the other person to do something, typically respond in some way. They're bits of information that beg the other person to grab hold of them.

Takers can take the limelight, but in doing so they create affordances and doorknobs on to which others can grab—the conversation really can flow. Questions are often (but not always) natural doorknobs, but any statement made that inspires the other person to jump in and take the floor, so to speak, is an affordance.

We can say that good conversationalists are always aware of the affordances they are creating for other people. They pepper their speech with little handles, pulleys, and levers so that the other person has something to reach out and grasp. With many doorknobs in a conversation, you can gather up energy and enthusiasm, enjoy rapid-fire give-and-take, and even interrupt enthusiastically (more on this later, but yes, there is some research suggesting that we like it when people are quick to respond to us—"*Fast response times signal social connection in conversation*" [Templeton et al. 2022]).

In an earlier chapter, we saw how questions like "What have you got planned for the weekend?" are actually unlikely to get a good conversational buzz going. The theory of affordance can explain why: Some questions or comments are just too *smooth*—we may feel that we're being awfully polite and generous by asking people these questions, but the truth is that they do not inspire us to rush in and answer. Consider this:

"I really love rock music. I was just at a concert the other day. My favorite bands are X, Y, and Z. Who are your favorite rock bands?"

This is really just a way of putting a question mark on the end of your own opinion/contribution and pretending it's an invitation for the other person to share. It's a little like asking, "Enough about me and what I like. I'm going to give you a chance to talk now . . . about what I like." Again, it's a question of empathy. Do you have reason to believe that the other person *wants* to talk about rock bands or any bands at all? If someone asked you this question, would you feel instantly compelled to answer? Chances are, it may feel like a bit of a chore. Small talk that feels tedious, insincere, or a little shallow often feels this way because there are no doorknobs. Asking someone, "Hey, what are your hobbies?" is not, in fact, a kind gesture likely to be met with enthusiasm, but almost like a tedious obligation, as though you were saying, "I'm going to ask this generic question, and now it's *your* job to say something entertaining. Go."

Balanced conversations are an art form. Adding more flow and dynamism to conversation is often just a question of knowing how to offer and accept conversational affordances.

Both giving and taking in a conversation should involve providing genuine opportunities for further dialogue. This means making statements or asking questions that invite responses and engagement from the other party. It's always great to ask a question, but a question is not automatically a "doorknob." Consider:

Question 1: "When does your course finish?"

Question 2: "Ooh, so what made you decide to do a first aid course?"

If you have trouble seeing which of the above questions creates more affordances, simply imagine the likely response given to each and how that would play out in a conversation. Some questions act like stop signs. The only way forward is to . . . ask another question. You could quickly end up in boring interview territory.

A conversational "taker" may say, "First aid, huh? That sounds interesting. Personally, I'm always the one causing the accidents . . ."

On its face, this is an egocentric answer, right? It brings attention back to the speaker and doesn't ask the other person anything about themselves. However, imagine that you've just told someone about your first aid course. Which response would give *you* more to work with—this one or "When does your course finish?"

By the same token, learning to notice affordances means knowing when one is being offered to *you*. Stay playful and curious, and when you notice someone sending you a conversational invitation, respond as quickly as you can.

Person A: "First aid, huh? That sounds interesting. Personally, I'm always the one causing the accidents . . ."

Person B: "Oh, are you? That's good news. Will you give me a call the next time you're choking? I need to practice my CPR!"

The next time you're in a casual conversation, practice listening closely for conversational cues. Notice who is in the limelight and when, and your own ratio of giving and taking. You don't have to politely and formally wait until someone asks you a question in order to contribute. And you can invite someone else's contribution without asking them a deliberate question—simply imagine throwing out a comment that begs to be picked up on. You will create an interaction that is a hundred times more authentic and enjoyable than a plodding question-and-answer session.

Interrupting

The psychology of interrupting appears straightforward: One person speaking is abruptly cut off by another, leaving the initial speaker resentful. Interruptions, however, are more nuanced than this initial observation suggests.

An interruption in conversation happens when one speaker cannot complete their sentence because they're interrupted by another person, who then begins their statement. The interrupted speaker is halted mid-thought, and their voice fades after the interruption point.

For instance:

Person A: I went to Disneyland [last week.]

Person B: [I love] Disneyland. It's my favorite place to hang out with my family.

Here, A is interrupted after mentioning "Disneyland." A slows down to allow room for B's interruption, and "last week" and "I love" are spoken simultaneously, as denoted by square brackets.

Pretty annoying, right? Or is it?

People interrupt for various reasons, and communication researcher Julia A. Goldberg believes that not all interrupting is created equal. She classifies interruptions into three main types:

Power interruptions: These interruptions occur when the interrupter seeks to actively gain control over the conversation, often to appear superior to the audience. Power interruptions are deliberate attempts to dominate the conversation, leading the interrupted party to feel disrespected and violated. Strategies for responding to power interruptions include tactfully re-asserting one's power and avoiding allowing the interrupter to take over the conversation.

Rapport interruptions: Designed to build rapport, these interruptions contribute positively to the conversation by showing that the speaker is heard and understood. Unlike power interruptions, rapport interruptions maintain a natural flow in the conversation and leave both parties feeling heard and respected. In fact, as we saw earlier, sometimes an interruption made out of enthusiasm can actually bolster rapport.

Neutral interruptions: These interruptions aren't aimed at gaining power or building rapport but may be misperceived as power interruptions. Reasons for neutral interruptions include being excited or emotional, differences in communication styles, attending to something more important, and mental health conditions such as Autism and ADHD. Importantly, there may be cultural differences and expectations around how to show a speaker that you are listening and supportive. Attention to nonverbal cues can help distinguish between power and neutral interruptions.

Interruptions in conversation, if done in the wrong spirit, often yield negative consequences for proper communication. Interrupting means you risk missing crucial information, but it also sends a clear message to the other person that you not only think of conversation as a competition, but that you are actively trying to win!

While occasional "crosstalk" is only natural and a sign of organic dialogue, frequent interruptions can lead to frustration, anger, or total communication breakdown. Generally, abrupt interruptions are only deemed appropriate during emergencies, when addressing insults, or when quickly seeking clarification. Even in these instances, however, it is crucial to interrupt *politely* and considerately to minimize any sense of disruption.

Interrupting people can be done tactfully with the right timing and tools. Here are a few ways to interrupt properly:

Watch Your Timing

Pay attention to the speaker's use of filler words such as "um," "like," or "you know." These are cues that they may be pausing and uncertain about their next thought, making it a suitable moment for interruption. Also notice the pauses between breaths, especially when guests are unsure about their next point. Interrupting during these natural breaks can be less jarring and more acceptable.

You can watch carefully for an obvious pause in the topic or a natural end to a particular thread. You may also choose to wait for a natural interruption from the environment— for example, a waiter coming to take an order (also a perfect time to interrupt with a "proposing" statement).

Use the "React Recap" Technique

Interrupt with a reaction, such as saying "Wait!" or "Hold on," followed by a recap of what was just mentioned, and then a question.

"Oh, hang on a second, so they told you the *dog* was going to be a ring bearer . . . I can't believe it. Is he going to wear a suit?"

This technique shows enthusiasm and interest, making the interruption feel inviting rather than intrusive. It also eases in your comment/question, because the recap shows that you are in fact listening to and acknowledging what you've heard, and not just blindly blurting out your own idea.

You can also try using small gestures, expressions, or sounds to signal that you are, in effect, "raising your hand" to speak, just like you did in school. Leaning in closer, opening your mouth, taking a breath as though to speak, or lifting a finger can all alert the other person to the fact that you're intending to interrupt. Pay attention to what happens, though—if the other person immediately starts speaking more loudly or more quickly, or does anything to suggest they don't want you to jump in, then don't!

Remember, the goal is to interrupt to encourage more from the other speaker, not to overshadow them or undermine them.

Be a Loud Listener

"Loud listening" is a term that refers to all those actions taken by listeners to let speakers know that they are being heard and understood. These actions can include vocal expressions like "Uh huh" and "Hm," but also facial expressions, gestures like nodding, leaning in closer, and any body language that suggests a visceral reaction to what they're being told.

There may well be individual differences in exactly how to do this, or indeed how much of it to do. Some cultures expect quite lively engagement from an audience and would interpret stone-cold silence as a lack of care or attention, rather than a sign of respect. Other cultures are the reverse. Men and women may differ from one another in this respect, too, just like people from different backgrounds or age groups.

The key here is to be aware that certain interjections can be classed as "supportive interrupting." Carefully consider the context, the person in front of you, and the topic at hand before making assumptions. A good rule of thumb is to listen closely for important emotional shifts in the speaker's message, and react in ways that demonstrate you've internalized this message: Laugh and smile at the punchline, scowl when you hear the bad news, and say, "No!" and, "*Really*?" when people relate an unbelievable detail. You get the idea.

You can also practice repeating key information back to the speaker to signal your support—it's a little like saying "Amen!" during a rousing sermon! You're not interrupting but showing that the conversation has moved you in some way. Finally, you can also use eye contact as a means of demonstrating your attentive listening. Make eye contact at the most important or pivotal moments, or when the other person is sharing key emotional insight.

What about if *you're* the one who is interrupted? The same principles apply—try to distinguish between someone trying to deliberately take control of the interaction versus someone who is merely enthusiastic or trying to show their support. If it is the case that someone is trying to dominate, there are plenty of graceful ways to assert yourself without damaging rapport.

Speak up—generally, the sooner you do, the better. "Oh, sorry, I wasn't finished speaking yet! As I was saying . . ." should do the trick. Try to avoid simply continuing to speak over them, as you will only find yourself in a battle of wills—and they won't be listening anyway. Keep it light and playful and treat the interjection as a harmless accident, rather than acting personally wounded. It should be more like "Oops, look what happened!" rather than "How dare you."

Occasionally you'll find yourself stuck with someone who simply refuses to let you speak. Unfortunately, you can have the best social skills in the world and be a phenomenal conversationalist, but none of it will matter if you're talking to a person who won't reciprocate. Don't worry too much; try to extricate yourself from these kinds of conversations without taking it personally. There are no prizes in life for enduring awful conversations, so just make your excuses and leave!

Getting Out of WTF Moments in Conversations

Now, speaking of cutting your losses and knowing when to abandon a conversation that just isn't working, we will end our book on a troubleshooting note. What do you do when an interaction is just plain old . . . wrong?

We've all experienced these moments before. They can be frustrating, confusing, annoying, even a little depressing. You're doing your best to reach the other person, and they're clearly trying to do the same, but something just isn't working. It's like you're speaking two different languages, and you're stuck. Perhaps you've landed in a full-blown misunderstanding that you can't make head or tail of, or maybe it's more subtle and you think, "How did we end up talking about *this*?"

There's a lot of discussion about conflict in communication, but there are infinite shades of grey before you reach conflict—an endless sea of potential weirdness, lack of understanding, and just the feeling that you're no longer making sense to one another. Let's call these "WTF moments."

Conversations can get stuck when there's a disconnect between what one person is trying to communicate and how the other person perceives it. This can happen even when discussing straightforward topics like deadlines, feedback, or work tasks—you are suddenly made very aware that other people really are their own universes, and that you cannot make an assumption about how they make meaning, what their goals and values are, or how they see *you* in the interaction.

First things first: relax. Really! Having this kind of lapse or break in communication is actually way more common than it might feel in the moment. Take a second to remind yourself that it's nobody's fault, and that it isn't necessarily a problem. Now is your chance to put your growing social skills to the test.

Step 1: Realize You're in It

The first step in addressing the "WTF moment" is to recognize that you're actually experiencing one. Realizing that something is going wrong is usually a fear trigger for people—we all worry that we have lost connection, that we don't belong, that we have caused offense, or that somehow we are not being accepted or understood. These can be very real and uncomfortable feelings.

If you allow yourself to lead with this fear, however, you may only become more attached to your personal point of view and even less able to see what is going wrong in order to address it. You will act defensively or to protect yourself and may resort to repeating the same thing over and over, leading to even more pronounced dead ends ("Oh, I give up! Do what you want. I don't care.")

Once you realize you've been emotionally triggered, you have a choice: shut down and cling even more to your perspective, or relax a little and become curious about how to get out of the swamp, so to speak.

Step 2: Genuinely Decide to Understand

It's a strange way to phrase it, isn't it? But you can *decide* to understand, just as you can decide that no matter what, you will not allow yourself to be budged. Shift your mindset to one of genuine curiosity. Decide to understand the other person's perspective by asking open questions that invite conversation rather than closed-ended questions that close off dialogue or force your perspective. Listen actively with the intention of understanding, not just waiting for the other person to finish speaking.

During conflicts and misunderstandings, the main problem is that there is a lack of relevant information. The other person is suddenly like a black box to you—something is going on inside their head, but you don't know what it is. Likely they feel that way about you. The only way to get a hold of that information is to *ask them* (not to assume or guess!).

Asking open-ended questions will not only give you access to that information, but it will signal that you care about finding it out in the first place. Own up to your own confusion and genuinely seek to understand. "I'm sorry, I'm just not getting this. What did you understand by that email? Can you explain to me exactly what you believe it meant?" The key is to do this in a neutral and sincere way.

Step 3: Repeat Until Some Piece of Shared Understanding Appears

Chances are you go round and round for a little while—you don't get a car unstuck from the mud on the first attempt. Continue asking open questions and listening patiently until you reach some level of shared understanding. Assume that it *is* there, and just keep changing tack until you discover what it might be.

Yes, this may take time and effort, but it's essential for moving the conversation forward and resolving the break. Be willing to accept that it is also your own filters, assumptions, and ego that may be getting in the way. Avoid listening with the intention that the other person is wrong. If you keep *insisting* that they don't make sense and are being difficult, for example, you cannot possibly hear all the ways they are trying to explain themselves and be conciliatory, right?

Be patient, stay receptive, and avoid making premature diagnoses and declarations about what the other person is saying or what they mean. Tread very carefully and slowly, and use phrases like "It sounds like you're saying X . . . Have I got that right?" Find some tiny seed that you can agree on, and then build on that.

If necessary, acknowledge when the conversation needs to end without reaching complete understanding. It's okay to say, "Let's set this aside for a moment to cool off, and come back to it later. What do you think?" Just ensure that you've made sincere efforts to connect and understand the other person's perspective.

Use the Process Move Out of Conflict

The concept of a "process move" comes from the world of chess. The idea is that you make careful, strategic moves to win the game. In conversation, however, your strategic moves are there to help *everyone* win.

A conversational process move is simple: Make an observation about how the process of conversation itself has become stuck or gone off track. This kind of meta observation is the kind of thing you'd offer in the "relational conversation" we discussed in a previous section. It's a way to step outside the misunderstanding or deadlock and draw attention to the dynamic itself.

Sometimes the observation alone can be helpful. When we're emotionally triggered, we may want to rush in immediately and solve the problem—or at least, what we believe the problem to be. But there is also value in just pausing, acknowledging the disconnect, and drawing neutral attention to it.

For example, if the conversation seems to be going in circles, you might say, "I'm noticing that we don't seem to be getting anywhere with this, and I wonder what we could do about that." That's it. You don't have to offer a solution, get emotional, or start placing blame. Just signal that you are aware of what's going on, and you're taking a step back. This simple observation has the power to shift the conversation dynamics significantly, partly because it allows for some distance from the problem at hand.

Using process moves may feel unfamiliar at first because they're not your everyday conversational fare and can feel a little phony. Done with assertiveness and confidence, however, such a move can convey transparency and a willingness to cooperate— and even when two people can't understand each other, they can still recognize the *intention* and *willingness* to understand.

To help you integrate process moves into your communication toolkit, here are some useful phrases you can experiment with:

"I'm noticing that we seem to be . . . (e.g., misunderstanding each other, getting stuck)."

"It feels like we are having two different conversations: You're talking about X and I'm talking about Y. What do *you* think is happening here?"

"It sounds like we're both finding it difficult to budge right now. I wonder what we could do to shift things?"

And for situations where tensions have escalated:

"I'm not sure we're getting anywhere with this conversation. I suggest we take a break and maybe come back to this later when we've both had a chance to calm down. Perhaps we can both think about what we want from this conversation moving forward."

Remember that even though you may be feeling frustrated, the thing that you most want to communicate is not your frustration, but your willingness to find some kind of resolution or understanding. That means that tone is important—choose your words carefully and use both verbal *and* nonverbal language that expresses openness and the absence of threat (for example, palms up and open hands, leaning forward, listening genuinely, and nodding).

Easing Out of Awkwardness

Of course, sometimes there's no major conflict or obvious problem—the interaction has just gone *weird*. We began our small talk journey with awkwardness and that's where we'll end.

Maybe you've just asked a woman who isn't pregnant when she was due. Maybe you made a joke to a second-language speaker that they didn't understand or hear properly, and now things are uncomfortable. Maybe there's just been a clumsy attempt at flirtation that crashed and burned.

There could be many reasons for a conversation suddenly withering and dying, but don't worry, it happens to everyone. There just may not be enough of a shared frame of reference, or you may have caught one another on a bad day. Sometimes a misstep can be relatively minor, yet it can feel hard to move on from, and trying to regain your previous momentum can actually add to the awkwardness.

Remind yourself that these glitches and low ebbs are normal. Even good friends, soul mates, and ultra-close family members have them now and again! If the "vibe" just isn't working and the chemistry is all off, there's nothing wrong with calling it a day and moving on. Humor can go a long way, as can a little self-deprecating joke. If the interaction really has gone a bit sour, there can be a lot of relief in just acknowledging this without freaking out or making it the other person's problem. Just shake it off and move on as quickly as possible.

Like mistakes in general, conversational blunders and missteps are best handled by acknowledging them as soon as possible and then gracefully backing away—don't dig in your heels, which tends to only make things worse.

"Oh, wow, I really embarrassed myself there, didn't I?"

"You know what, it seems like we're both a little tired this evening, huh? What do you say we call this a night and pick this up some other time?"

"Oh no, that's not what I meant, sorry. Never mind, it's not important. Have a great day, okay?" (paired with a big smile).

Remember that vulnerability can actually create more closeness and smooth over any minor embarrassments. Handled well, a dud joke or a weird disconnect can sometimes be turned around and become an opportunity to connect more deeply. Be real, be kind (including to yourself), and if a conversation suddenly flops, it's okay! Just let it go and learn for next time.

Summary:

- Conversations can and do go wrong. Relax! There is always a way out. Empathy means understanding the experiences, perceptions, and feelings of another person, but can be difficult if our anxiety makes us self-absorbed.
- Another issue is an empathy mismatch. There are three empathy types: cognitive, emotional, and compassionate. Understand the difference between them and be mindful of which kind is required. Empathy is not something you feel, but a message you actively communicate to someone else, primarily for their benefit.
- Avoid platitudes, advice, or centering yourself when being empathetic, and instead try the following formula: [Reflect their experience by labeling their emotion and link it to a reason] + [Expression of feeling] + [Thoughtful question, suggestion, or offer of help].
- In conversations, "givers" and "takers" refer to different approaches that people adopt when engaging with others; givers give the "spotlight," while takers take it— both have their value, but a mismatch can

prove problematic. Pay attention to the flow and balance of give-and-take and adjust accordingly.

- The key is finding a **balance** between giving and taking, offering and accepting conversational affordances or "doorknobs" that other people can grab hold of. Good conversationalists are always aware of the affordances they are creating for other people, and they strive for balance and flow for everyone involved. Stay playful and listen for conversational cues.
- There are different types of interrupting— power, rapport, and neutral. Be aware of the differences and pay attention to how interrupting could be helping or hindering. Watch your timing, use the "react recap" formula, and practice being a loud listener.
- Don't worry about glitches, flops, or weirdness in conversations. "WTF" moments are normal. Realize that a lapse has happened and genuinely seek to understand, looking for common ground or a point of understanding. A "process move" can help, but you can always just move on. Don't take it too seriously!

Printed in Great Britain
by Amazon